Letting Residential Property

A Practical Guide for Owners

Frances M Way

KOGAN PAGE

The law of property is constantly being reviewed and changed. The law stated relates to England and Wales only. The law is stated as at the time of going to press. Kogan Page Ltd and the author cannot assume legal responsibility for the accuracy of any particular statement in this work. The reader should seek legal advice from a solicitor which is tailored to his individual needs and those of the property. No responsibility for loss or damage occasioned to any person acting or refraining from action as a result of the material in this publication can be accepted by the author or publisher.

The masculine pronoun has been used throughout this book. This stems from a desire to avoid cumbersome language, and no discrimination, prejudice or bias is intended.

First published in 1993, reprinted 1995

Apart from any fair dealing for the purposes of research or private study, or criticism or review, as permitted under the Copyright, Designs and Patents Act, 1988, this publication may only be reproduced, stored or transmitted, in any form or by any means, with the prior permission in writing of the publishers, or in the case of reprographic reproduction in accordance with the terms of licences issued by the Copyright Licensing Agency. Enquiries concerning reproduction outside those terms should be sent to the publishers at the undermentioned address:

Kogan Page Limited
120 Pentonville Road
London N1 9JN

© Frances M Way 1993

British Library Cataloguing in Publication Data
A CIP record for this book is available from the British Library.
ISBN 0–7494–0973–8

Printed in England by Clays Ltd, St Ives plc

Contents

1 **Should you let your property?**   9
Why let your property? 9; Using a solicitor 11; Using an estate agent or letting agent 12; Do you need an accountant? 13; Ready reckoner 13; Tax 15; Stamp duty 16

2 **What is a tenancy?**   17
Freehold and leasehold 17; Different types of lease 19; What is security of tenure? 22; Licences 23; Why a tenancy should be in writing 24

3 **Letting a room in your own home**   27
Initial considerations 27; The type of letting 29; Sensible rules for a peaceful life 32; Your personal relationship with your house-mate 36

4 **Letting a whole house or flat: the theory**   38
How the Housing Act 1988 affects you and your tenant 38; Assured tenancies and assured shorthold tenancies 39; What happens if the tenant wants to leave? 42; How to create an assured

tenancy 43; How to create an assured shorthold tenancy 43; Letting your own home 44

5 **Letting a whole house or flat: the practice**   46
Suitability of the property for the type of letting 46; Rent 47; Personal preferences for individual or group lettings 47; Lease or licence? 49

6 **Responsibilities of landlord and tenant and licensor and licensee**   52
Maintenance and repair 52; Decorating 55; Alterations 55; Assignment and sub-letting 55; Use of the property 57; Being a nuisance or annoyance to others 57; Fitness for habitation 57; Provision of fire escapes and equipment 58; Furniture 59; Bills 59; Why these terms and conditions are useful 60

7 **Letting a block of flats or a conversion**   62
Planning the letting 62; Service charges 63; Other arrangements 67; Insurance 67; Proper management of flats 67; Right to buy the freehold 68

8 **Managing the property**   69
Preparing the property for letting 69; Consulting a solicitor and/or an estate agent 71; Setting the rent or licence fee 72; Collecting the rent or licence fee 73; Deposits 74; Sureties 74; Advertising the property 74; Showing the property 75; Choosing a tenant 76; When the tenant moves in 77; 'DSS' tenants 78; Maintaining the property 79; Increasing the rent 79

9 **Termination and renewal**   84
Termination by the tenant 84; Assured

tenancies – termination by the landlord 85; The grounds for possession 86; Mandatory grounds 87; Discretionary grounds 90; Assured shorthold tenancies – termination by the landlord 92; Practical aspects of terminating a tenancy 94; Renewing a tenancy 96; Terminating a tenancy or licence which is not under the Housing Act 98; What if the tenant or licensee wants to quit? 100; Renewal of the tenancy or licence 100

10 **Problem tenants and licensees** 101
Rent or licence fee problems 101; Breach of covenant 107; Causing a nuisance 109; Harassment and eviction 109; Summary 112

Glossary 113

Index 126

CHAPTER 1

Should you let your property?

Many people think about letting their property but are put off by the fear that being a landlord involves too many responsibilities and having tenants is bound to cause problems. This book will show you that such fears may be unjustified and that, with proper care and forethought, letting can be an enjoyable and profitable use of property.

As long as you consider the practical implications of letting the sort of property you have in mind – whether that is a whole house or just a room in your own flat – and provided a suitable type of tenancy arrangement is made in writing, a good landlord and tenant relationship may be established that is mutually rewarding. A 'Ready Reckoner' or series of questions designed to help you decide whether letting your property is suitable for you is given at the end of this chapter.

Why let your property?

There are many reasons why you might want to let your property rather than sell it or even let it stand unused.

- You may have a spare room in your own house and would like to let it to an individual to make an extra income. Alternatively, you may be thinking of turning part of your house into a separate flat.
- If you expect to be away from your home for a considerable

time, perhaps on business or on holiday, letting your house can be a good way of making your property work for you as well as ensuring that the house does not stand empty and uncared for.

- If you have a second home which you no longer use very frequently, letting it will provide you with an income and give you time to decide whether to sell the property. Alternatively, you may have inherited property and be unable to decide what to do with it; letting it will give you time to think, and may be a long-term solution in itself.

- You may wish to acquire some property and let it as a capital investment.

- You may need to move house but be unable to sell your old house quickly enough, or be unable to sell it for the price you want owing to the current state of the property market; letting may be a good interim solution.

- If your son or daughter is leaving home, you may be thinking of buying them a place to live in. Renting spare rooms to friends can provide a handy source of income or help to cover the cost of the purchase.

If the total outlay involved can be recovered reasonably quickly from the rent, letting property can be both a profitable and a neat solution to many situations. Letting will enable you to keep hold of the property as a capital investment which may be realised in the future, but will also provide you with an income in the meantime which should cover the costs of letting and provide you with further capital which you could invest or use. You will have the freedom to realise that capital investment when you decide that the property market is favourable to you and also according to your own personal needs. Alternatively, you may decide to invest the proceeds from letting into buying more property to build up a property portfolio which may be a valuable business to run or to sell at a later date.

It may be that you are unsure about whether to sell the property or move into it yourself later on – letting the property will give you the time to make this decision. Letting may also be a good long-term source of steady income, or a good way of using property which you would like to leave to someone in your will.

This book will consider in detail the different types of situation

SHOULD YOU LET YOUR PROPERTY?

a landlord might be in, and how to tailor the tenancy to suit your needs. For example, the person who wants to let a spare room in their own house, largely to help make ends meet, will have very different things to consider than the person who has a whole house standing empty. Both the legal and practical considerations of letting and managing the type of property you have in mind will be dealt with.

Each chapter will consider different types of letting and how to ensure that you do not encounter problems. However, should unforeseen events occur, Chapter 10 deals with what can be done if, for example, the tenant has not paid the rent, has damaged furniture or is causing a nuisance. Although this book will explain that proper forethought can prevent these situations occurring in the first place or that they can be solved without resorting to using the law, the various legal options will also be considered.

Since the Housing Act 1988 was introduced, letting residential property has become much easier. The Act was passed in order to revitalise the private rented residential sector by enabling landlords to let their property at market rates, secure in the knowledge that the tenancy could be brought to an end. The legal aspects of letting property will be considered without using technical jargon so that you know your rights and responsibilities and the tenant's rights and responsibilities.

Using a solicitor

No book, however, can be a substitute for seeking proper legal advice, and it must be emphasised that it is very important to draw up a suitable written tenancy agreement which takes into account all the aspects of the tenancy.

You may need to approach several advisers, such as a solicitor, an accountant, and an estate agent or letting agent. As with most things, it is always worth shopping around and enquiring about what costs are likely to be involved and, in the case of estate or letting agents, the amount of commission that will be levied on the rent, if any.

A solicitor will advise you what sort of tenancy you should consider, and will deal with any queries that you may have. Obviously, if you have a good understanding of the sort of tenancy you have in mind, and know the right sort of questions to ask, your solicitor will be able to advise you more easily (and therefore cheaply). Instead of responding to problems when they occur, you will be able to plan in advance with your solicitor to avoid those problems in the first place. Your solicitor will also draft the tenancy agreement. The glossary explains the common legal terminology used and what it means. The tenant may want to change some of the terms, and your solicitor will be able to negotiate this on your behalf. When you come to let the property again, the costs should be cheaper as the tenancy agreement should be substantially the same.

If you intend to use an estate agent to let the property, the estate agent will usually have a standard tenancy agreement which he can alter to suit the particular property and the needs of the parties. However, even if you do use the estate agent's standard tenancy agreement, the landlord should still obtain proper legal advice as these agreements are not self-explanatory, and it is important to ensure that they are completely up to date with the law.

Using an estate agent or letting agent

An estate agent or letting agent can assist you in advertising the property for rent and can also take over the management of the property if you so wish. The agent's fee will be a proportion of the monthly rent – again, it is worth shopping around. As agents usually only receive a fee once they have successfully let the property, they will have a good incentive to advertise the property widely and negotiate as good a rent as possible. However, it is worth asking very detailed questions about how the property will be advertised and where, and what sort of would-be tenants will be reached by this advertising.

An agent will usually also answer enquiries about the property and arrange to show prospective tenants around. You should decide whether you wish to be present as well so that you can meet the prospective tenants and if so, you should tell the agent what times of the day would be convenient for you. Once a tenant has agreed to rent the property, the agent will usually see to such details as getting the contract signed, supplying the tenant with keys, reading the gas and electricity meters, and checking the inventory of the fixtures and fittings. Using an agent may therefore be sensible if you do not have the time to attend to these details yourself.

It would also be a good idea to ask an agent to manage the day-to-day running of the property if you are going to be away from the area for a considerable time or if you have several properties to let and need help in managing them. The agent will respond to all enquiries from the tenant, collect rent and arrange repairs. Another option may be to ask a trusted friend to take over this part of the agent's role.

Do you need an accountant?

If you are intending to make a substantial income from letting, or if you will be running your own business letting property, an accountant would be able to advise you about the mechanics of running a business, such as whether to be a sole trader or to set up a limited company, how much tax you should pay, and what costs of letting the property may be set off against your tax. Income from rents must, of course, be notified to the Inland Revenue, and an accountant will be able to help you produce your annual accounts and your tax return for the Inland Revenue.

Ready reckoner

Practical considerations
1. How long will it be possible to let the property for?

- A minimum of six months is necessary in order to create an assured shorthold tenancy (see page 39). Although other forms of agreement may be for a shorter period, it could be difficult to attract a tenant to stay for such a short time.

- It is administratively easier and cheaper to let property for a longer period.

2. If you are letting a room in your own house:

- Is your property suitable for sharing communal rooms, such as the kitchen, bathroom and living room? Or are there separate ones for the tenant?

- Will this arrangement suit your life style?
- Is the room big enough to attract the sort of tenant you wish to share your house with (for example, a student would need space to study)?

3. If you are letting a house or flat:
- How will you see to the management of the property (for example, are you able to oversee the property yourself, or will it be necessary to ask a friend or employ an agent)?
- Is the property suitably furnished or do you have the funds necessary to furnish them to a satisfactory standard? Alternatively, do you wish to let the property unfurnished?

4. Is the property mortgaged? If so, you will need to obtain your bank or building society's consent to the letting and they may charge you a slightly higher interest rate on your mortgage.

Income
1. How much rent can you charge?
- Consult local newspapers and estate agents to determine the market rent for the sort of property you are letting.
- Remember to allow for times that the property or individually let rooms in the property may be left unlet, and to allow for income tax (see page 15).

2. Annual service charge
- A service charge is sometimes set to recoup costs of general maintenance, or you may include this amount in the rent you set (see pages 63-6).

Expenditure
These should be calculated on an annual basis:
- Cost of furnishing the premises to a suitable standard.
- Estimated cost of using an agent to advertise the property or cost of advertising property in newspapers, shop windows etc.
- Estimated solicitor's fees.
- Cost of repairing the property. You should consider the char-

SHOULD YOU LET YOUR PROPERTY?

acter of the specific property as an older house will probably need more attention than a new house. Consider the repairs that you have found necessary to make to the property or a similar property in the past.

- Cost of maintaining the garden if this is not to be the tenant's responsibility.
- Cost of maintaining communal areas in flats, such as lighting and cleaning stairways and entrances, maintaining the lift.
- Cost of insuring the property and the fixtures and fittings provided by you.
- Incidental expenses such as dry cleaning fittings after the end of tenancies, postage and telephone.

Tax

Money from letting property is income and must be notified to the tax office. There are some differences if the property is unfurnished or furnished.

- If the property is unfurnished, the tax is based on the *rent due*, whether or not the rent was actually received. If the rent was not received, you would have to plead for this rule to be waived and show that you tried to recover the rent.
- If the property is furnished, the tax is based on the *rent actually received*. If services are provided, such as cleaning, meals and laundry, money received for these services is treated as income from self-employment.

Certain expenses incurred in connection with letting the property can be set off against the tax. For example:

- repairs and redecorations carried out while the property is being let and which are necessary due to wear and tear;
- money spent by the landlord on lighting and maintaining the common areas;
- heating and lighting the tenant's property if the tenant is not responsible for this;
- services provided to the tenant by the landlord at no extra cost, such as maintaining the garden;

- water rates payable by the landlord;
- insurance premiums payable by the landlord.

There is also a special scheme, known as the 'rent a room' scheme, which offers the landlord tax relief:

- The landlord must be letting his only or main residential furnished home, and the landlord must be an owner occupier, or a tenant who has the right to sub-let the property.
- Rent received up to £3,250 (1993 figure) in any one tax year will not be liable for income tax.
- If the rent received is more than this figure, the landlord can elect *either* to pay tax on the gross rent which exceeds £3,250 with no expenses allowed, *or* to pay tax on the whole rent with expenses allowed.
- If the landlords are husband and wife, they can choose whether one claims the relief, or whether it is divided between them.

Stamp duty

Stamp duty is a voluntary tax in that you can decide whether or not you want to pay it, but there is really little choice. If you do not pay stamp duty, the agreement will not be allowed as valid evidence in court. The duty should be paid within 30 days of the agreement being made, but late payment with a penalty payment can be made. Once the duty has been paid, the agreement will be stamped as proof of payment.

The amount of duty varies according to the length of the lease and whether or not the property is furnished. If the lease is for seven years or less, or if it is indefinite because it is periodic (such as monthly) and the rent is more than £500 per year, the duty is 50 pence per £50 (or part thereof) of the annual rent.

For furnished lettings where the lease is less than one year long and the total rent is more than £500, there is a flat rate duty of £1. If the property is unfurnished and let for less than one year, the duty is 1 per cent of the rent. (All prices and calculations are at 1993 levels).

CHAPTER 2

What is a tenancy?

The more you understand about what is involved in letting property, the more you will be in control of your business. This chapter will introduce and demystify several pieces of legal terminology so that you can play a greater part in the decision-making process with your legal adviser. You do not need to be a legal eagle to let property successfully, but if you understand some of the basics of the law, which is in essence quite simple, you will have a better feel for your business. Most importantly, you should be able to avoid problems arising from oversight, vagueness or lack of knowledge. Instead you will have the confidence to manage your letting knowing that you are within your rights.

All too often tenancies come into existence because of some informal arrangement. The parties involved are usually unaware of the nature of the tenancy until some problem arises, for example the occupier stops paying rent, or the owner neglects to repair the property. The parties have only themselves to blame, because creating a proper tenancy before it begins is the ideal opportunity to regulate the relationship between the owner and occupier. It is important to be in full control of letting the property from the outset, and to be aware of the rights and obligations of both parties.

Freehold and leasehold

It is useful to know a little about these two distinct ways of owning property. If you own the freehold of a property, you own it 'outright' and are free to do with it as you will within the law. A leasehold property is owned only for a certain time as the lease will eventually come to an end. This may not be an important distinction if you have a long lease. Leases of 999 years are quite common. However, if you have a lease, someone else will have a greater or 'superior' ownership or 'interest' in the property as the lease will have been granted to you by someone who owns the freehold, or by someone who has a longer lease than you. Unlike a freeholder, a leaseholder is not free to do with the property as he likes because the leaseholder's relationship with the person owning the superior interest will be governed by rules implied by the law and/or rules or 'covenants' made by agreement between the parties.

Both a freeholder and a leaseholder have an interest or right in the property. This ability to have an actual interest in the property is peculiar to land. With other things, such as a car, you can either own it, or have possession of it. For example, William owns a car, but lets Martin drive it. Although Martin has possession of the car, he has no rights to it and it remains fully owned by William. But if William owns a house and grants a lease of it to Martin, Martin has a right to the house or an 'interest' in it which is recognised by law, so that William cannot simply demand the house back when he feels like it. Martin would have no right to sell the car, but, unless they had agreed otherwise, Martin could sell his lease to someone else.

The property which you want to let may be either freehold or leasehold. If it is freehold, you will be the sole landlord. If it is leasehold, you will have a landlord and you and your solicitor must make sure that there are no covenants between you and your landlord which prevent you from leasing the property, or, if there are, that you have first obtained your landlord's consent to the letting. Your solicitor will also ensure that you do not grant your tenant rights which you are prevented from granting because of any covenant between you and your landlord. For example, you should not grant a right to let your tenant run a business from the property if your own lease prohibits you from running a business because, although you might not live in the property any more, you will still be bound by your covenants with your landlord. Generally, if you have a long lease of about 50 years or more, there will usually not be many restrictions on you.

If you own a flat, it is more than likely that you will have a lease rather than own the freehold, but here the lease is really more of a conveyancing device rather than a document creating a detailed landlord and tenant relationship. Although it is possible to have a freehold of a flat, or 'flying freehold' as they are known, it is often impractical. Covenants in leases can ensure that the whole block of flats is looked after properly by everyone. For example, a lease can stipulate that the ground floor occupier does not demolish the structural walls, and it can make all the flat owners responsible for keeping the roof in a good condition. Without these covenants, individual flat owners could find their property devalued or ruined, and for this reason, banks and building societies are reluctant to give mortgages to owners of a flying freehold. Flats are usually leaseholds rather than freeholds because the device of a lease is also a way of ensuring all the occupiers share common areas and contribute to their maintenance. Often the landlord remains the owner of the common area, such as the garden, or hallway, and charges the tenants for repairs and maintenance, or the landlord can grant a lease of the common areas to a specially created company or association (run by the tenants themselves or with the landlord) and the tenants pay money to the company or association. For more information on blocks of flats, see Chapter 7.

Owning a lease rather than a freehold is not necessarily a bar to letting your property. As long as you have a lease which has a reasonable length of time to run, you can grant a shorter lease, or sub-lease, assuming your lease does not prohibit you from doing this and you have obtained any necessary agreement from your landlord. However, the more onerous and detailed your own lease is, the more careful you and your solicitor will have to be when drafting the new lease, and it is also likely that, as your solicitor will have more work to do, the legal fees will be more expensive than for a freehold owner.

Different types of lease

There are several different types of lease and the following brief explanation is again by way of background only. This background is important on the grounds that prevention is better than cure, because there are some leases that you will want to avoid creating inadvertently. Chapters 3 to 5 deal in more detail with the specific types of tenancy that you are likely to find suitable.

Lease for a fixed term

This is a lease that specifies when it comes to an end. As you will want to be in control of your letting, you will want to create a lease for a certain length of time so that you know when you can bring the lease to an end. The lease can be for any length of time but it must end on a definite date. The length of time need not be continuous; for example, timeshares of holiday homes may specify 'the first two weeks of August each year for five years'.

Periodic lease

These leases are often created by accident! A periodic lease is one that has no definite end but instead continues running from one period to the next, such as from year to year, month to month, or week to week, until the lease is brought to an end by either landlord or tenant. Periodic leases can be created 'expressly', that is, you can make an agreement with your tenant that the lease is to be periodic. Often periodic leases are instead implied or deemed to exist by the law where there is no express agreement. For example, if you allow someone to move into your property without first making an agreement, but the tenant pays rent at regular intervals, there will be an implied periodic tenancy. The period of the tenancy is usually determined by the frequency with which the rent is paid. Therefore, if the rent is paid monthly, the lease is a monthly periodic lease. Or you could have weekly, quarterly, half yearly or yearly periodic leases accordingly.

A periodic lease also arises if someone has occupied the property under a fixed term lease which has expired, but the tenant continues to live there with the landlord's consent. The tenant will gain a periodic lease, and the period will usually be according to the frequency with which the rent is paid, and the terms of the lease will be the same as the fixed term lease. Such a tenant is said to be 'holding over' when their fixed term lease expires.

A periodic lease comes to an end when the landlord or tenant gives notice to the other that the lease is to end. The length of the notice must be for the same length of the period of the lease (except in the case of a yearly periodic lease which may be terminated on half a year's notice, specifying the date of termination as the end of the lease's year). The minimum period of notice is two weeks. Chapter 9 deals with terminating different types of lease in more detail. The amount of notice required to end a

WHAT IS A TENANCY?

periodic tenancy is one of the reasons why periodic leases can be irksome. Unless there was a previous agreed lease, the terms will all be implied by the law, and this can cause uncertainty and lead to disagreements.

Tenancy at will

This sort of tenancy is for no fixed period and arises when the tenant does not have an agreed lease, and does not pay any rent. As soon as rent is paid, the tenancy becomes a periodic lease. Either the landlord or the tenant can end the lease 'at will', that is, in effect whenever they like. The landlord would be entitled to 'compensation' in the form of money for the use of the property.

Tenancies at will are very dangerous because they can easily turn into periodic leases. For example:

> Angela thinks it would be a good idea to let her empty basement to Betty. They agree to 'sort everything out as friends rather than make any sort of formal arrangement'. Betty moves in one day but does not pay any rent for a while. A tenancy at will arises.
>
> Angela gets fed up and threatens to make Betty move out if she does not 'play fair' and pay some rent. Angela could tell Betty to go at any time, but before she gets around to it, Betty decides to pay Angela £50 a month. Angela accepts this as rent although she thinks it is a bit low, and immediately a monthly periodic tenancy arises. Angela has an argument with Betty, but now, because there is a monthly periodic tenancy, she has to give Betty a month's notice to leave. Betty tries to claim that she has security of tenure and cannot be asked to go (see pages 22–3).

Tenancy at sufferance

This is a very vague tenancy so far as the law is concerned. It exists where a lease has been brought to an end and the tenant stops paying rent, but the tenant stays on without either the landlord's acquiescence or disagreement (if the landlord did agree it would be a tenancy at will). A tenancy at sufferance is basically a term used to distinguish between a person who once entered the property under a valid lease and a trespasser who had no right to enter the property. If the landlord makes it known that he does not assent to the occupation, the occupier becomes a trespasser.

Short leases and long leases

A lease may be for any length of time – a week, a month, or 999 years, for example. There are several reasons for creating short leases, principally because of the different laws applying to short leases as compared to long leases, and also for practical convenience. A long lease, for the purposes of the law, is generally one which is for a period of 21 years or more. Owners of long leases have many rights created by statute such as continuing the tenancy beyond the expiry of the lease, and 'leasehold enfranchisement' which means that in some circumstances the tenant can purchase the freehold of the property from the landlord.

These consequences of creating a long lease are obviously undesirable for the landlord who wishes to run a successful small business letting property. Therefore this book concentrates on short leases.

The actual length of the lease will depend on many factors such as the availability of the property, and the needs of different types of tenant. For example, students and young people usually prefer short tenancies of six months to a year, whereas older people who are more settled in an area due to family and work commitments will be hoping to rent a place for a year or more. In this sort of market, people usually do not want to bind themselves to long leases of more than five years. Chapter 5 deals with these considerations in more detail (see pages 50–51).

What is security of tenure?

A lease actually creates an interest in and rights over the land itself rather than just being a personal contract between two parties. As a person's home is so important to that individual, various Acts of Parliament have from time to time created laws to ensure that the tenant has security of tenure, that is, the tenant has a right to remain in the property and can only be made to leave in specified circumstances, such as substantial rent arrears. Even then, the landlord would have to obtain an order from the court before the tenant could be made to vacate the property.

You may have heard of Rent Act protected tenancies (under the Rent Act 1977) and stories about landlords being forced to keep tenants, sometimes well beyond the date when the lease expired and at very low rents which did not cover the landlord's expenses.

Since the Housing Act 1988 was introduced, these sorts of tenancy are being phased out. As from 15 January 1989 it became impossible to create Rent Act protected tenancies.

The main reason why the Housing Act abolished these old tenancies is because the government thought that potential landlords were being discouraged from letting their property for fear that they would be stuck with problem tenants who enjoyed rents that were far below market value because they were set by rent tribunals. The new Act was introduced to revitalise the private rented housing sector but to ensure that tenants are still adequately protected.

One of the main effects of the new Act is that a landlord and tenant are able to agree a market rent for the property. Although the tenant can apply for the rent to be reviewed by a Rent Assessment Committee in some circumstances (see pages 79–83), the Committee will consider the going rate for the sort of property let to the tenant. The new Act also makes it easier and simpler to bring tenancies to an end (see pages 84–96).

The landlord can choose whether to create a tenancy which gives the tenant full security of tenure – an assured tenancy (the landlord must prove certain grounds or conditions before the tenancy is terminated) or an assured shorthold tenancy which offers security only for a limited amount of time. If the landlord fails to make a choice, the lease will be an assured tenancy. The Act protects the tenant by making it an offence if the landlord does not follow the correct procedures. These procedures are not particularly onerous and are explained in Chapters 8 and 9.

Licences

As we have seen, a lease creates an actual interest in the land itself. There is, however, another form of occupation which is known as a contractual licence. A licence is usually just a personal contract, which may be in writing or oral, made between the owner (the licensor) and the occupier (the licensee). The licence permits the licensee to be on the property; without the licensor's permission, the occupier would have no right to stay on the property and would be a trespasser.

A licence can be terminated by either party very easily and, except in very rare circumstances, a court would not permit the licensee to remain in the property once the licence had been properly terminated. A licensee has no security of tenure under the Housing Act 1988, and no right to have the licence fee, which is equivalent to rent, assessed. Like tenants, the licensee will be protected from harassment and unlawful eviction.

Obviously it would be very easy for landlords to avoid the provisions of the Housing Act by simply creating a licence rather than a lease. This is not possible because, whatever the landlord may choose to call the agreement, a court will come to its own conclusion as to whether the arrangement is a lease or licence. This is because a licence can only exist in certain circumstances. These circumstances are discussed on pages 29-32. Basically, for the agreement to be a licence, the occupier must have no right to exclusive possession of the property and have no right to prevent other people from entering it and sharing the facilities – lodgers who receive services with their room usually have licences.

The law

Although to a certain extent the landlord and tenant or licensor and licensee are free to make whatever terms they agree, they cannot make terms that the law does not allow them to make; if they do, those terms are void. In some cases, if the parties do not make an express agreement as to certain matters (such as repairs, assigning the lease, serving notice to quit) the law will 'fill in the gaps' or 'imply' terms into the agreement.

The law of property is partly statutory, that is by Act of Parliament, and partly governed by the common law, which is the law that has evolved over the centuries on certain principles decided by judges in court cases. Sometimes the common law and statutory law overlap. The only definitive interpretation of the law as it stands is that given by a court. New cases constantly change the common law and its interpretation, and the interpretation of statutory law. New statutes come into force, and old statutes are revised and repealed. For this reason, it is essential that owners and occupiers obtain up to date professional legal advice based on the particular facts of their case.

Why a tenancy should be in writing

In certain circumstances a lease or licence does not have to be in writing. The parties may make an oral agreement as to what the terms of the occupancy are, and these terms, as long as they do not contravene the law, will be valid and binding.

The obvious difficulty with oral agreements is that memories fade and it would be practically impossible to prove who really said what in the event of a disagreement. The parties might also forget to discuss some aspect of the agreement, such as whether the tenant is able to let someone else take his place by assigning or giving the tenancy to someone else. In this situation the law would fill in the gaps and say that there was an implied term permitting the tenant to assign (depending on the circumstances). Had the landlord thought about this first, he might well have decided to prohibit assignment. The court can also examine what happened in practice during the occupation in order to glean what the terms of the tenancy are. For example, if the landlord usually mows the lawn, it may be a term of the agreement that the landlord will tend the garden and the tenant need not share any of that responsibility even though he has use of the garden.

A very serious consequence of not putting the agreement in writing is that the very basis of the occupation could be uncertain – is it a lease or licence? What sort of lease is it? If it is a lease, is it governed by the Housing Act?

Putting a lease or licence in writing will take a bit of time, effort and money, but in the long run it will be well worth it. Both you and the occupier will know where you stand and this will reduce the likelihood of disagreements or problems. As we will see in later chapters, it is quite simple to build into the agreement terms that will discourage the occupier from falling into bad habits – a provision that interest is payable on late rent will help to ensure that rent is paid promptly, for example.

Sometimes a lease or licence can be created orally by mistake when the owner has the full intention of writing a proper agreement. An oral agreement may sometimes arise if you, or your agent, agree to terms of the occupation with the tenant or licensee and accept money for rent or the licence fee or allow the person to move in, before the agreement is drawn up and signed. You must therefore be careful to discuss terms only in principle and not be bound into any commitments before the document is agreed.

Any business must be properly organised if it is to be successful, and letting property, whether on a large or small scale, is no exception. It is common sense to put the agreement in writing, to consult professional advisers, to keep a record of correspondence and a note of important conversations (which should be confirmed in writing as well), and to keep accurate records of rent or licence fees received and expenses incurred. You may decide to delegate these responsibilities to a letting agent (for further information on managing property, see Chapter 8).

With a bit of planning, forethought and professional advice it is quite easy to be in full control of letting your property and create a successful business. The next chapter will help you to decide what will suit your property and your needs, and how to attract and keep the right sort of tenant or lodger for the property.

CHAPTER 3

Letting a room in your own home

Letting a room in your own home is probably the simplest sort of letting from a legal and managerial point of view. You have the advantage that you will be able to keep a close eye on the room and how the occupier uses it. As you will be living with someone at quite close quarters it is important to consider all the practical implications beforehand. This is important even if you know the person quite well, so that you both know where you stand and confusions and arguments can be avoided.

Initial considerations

Is the room adequate?
Take a good look around the room and think about whether it is suitable for the sort of person you would like to live there. For example, if you would like a student to move in, is there enough room for a desk and shelves for books?

The room should be comfortable and attractive enough so that the person will be able to settle in and feel at home, otherwise you could have a succession of people moving out which would be very disruptive both socially and financially. The room should be a good size, with adequate heating and lighting. The furniture should be in good repair, and offer enough storage space to keep personal belongings such as clothes and books.

Ideally the room should have:

- bed;
- wardrobe;
- chest of drawers;
- writing table or desk and chair;
- armchair;
- bookshelves;
- other usual furnishings such as carpet, curtains, radiator.

It is usual for the occupier to provide other items such as bed linen and towels, unless you are providing a laundry service.

Make a list of all the items of furniture you will need to buy and any repairs and decorations that you will need to make, and how much this will cost.

What other rooms will the occupier share?
The occupier will need access to a bathroom and toilet and kitchen. Unless you are able to offer separate facilities you and other members of your household will be sharing these facilities with the occupier. It is also quite common to permit the occupier to share the living room with you. If you would not like this, you should ensure that the occupier's own room is a suitable place to relax in and entertain friends. You should also decide whether you will allow access to the garden.

Think carefully about whether you and your household are happy about sharing these facilities with someone else, and indeed whether you are the sort of person someone would like to share a house with! You should make sure that sharing your home will fit in with your life style. For example, another person in the house is bound to make some noise – will this affect your work or your sleep?

Security and safety
Other things to consider before making the decision to let a room in your own home is the personal security of you and the occupier, and of the home and its contents. Your local police station should be able to advise you on these aspects and check your home.

Fitting window locks and a mortice lock and chain on the door are relatively cheap improvements to make and are well worth it. However, do also make sure that it is easy to escape from the house in the event of fire. It is sensible to invest in a couple of smoke alarms now if you have not already done so.

As you are the owner of the house and most of its contents, you must ensure that they are safe to use.

The occupier should be advised about security arrangements and instructed never to lend their key to anyone or get an extra key cut without your prior permission and never to allow friends to stay in the house when they are out.

As regards your own personal security, you should take extra care when selecting the person to whom you offer the room. Besides taking up all the references recommended on pages 76–77, it is worth trying to get to know the person beforehand. Find out as much as you can about the person to see if your life styles will be compatible. If a person has nothing to hide he will usually be quite happy to talk about himself.

Try to cover the following topics:

- why he is leaving his current address;
- how long he has lived in the area;
- what his long-term plans are;
- family and friends, boyfriend/girlfriend (as appropriate);
- hobbies and pastimes and how he spends the weekend;
- whether he is a smoker.

It is wise to arrange for comprehensive insurance of your home and contents if you have not already done so now that another person will be sharing the house. If you already have an insurance policy in place it is vital that you inform the insurance company that you are going to let part of your home as it is possible that your policy may become invalid if you do not do this. The occupier should arrange for insurance of his own personal belongings at his own expense.

The type of letting

The type of letting will depend on whether it is appropriate in the circumstances to give the occupier a lease or a licence.

Licences or lodgings

The advantage of creating a licence rather than a lease is that with a licence there is no security of tenure and no rent controls. As you will see, however, the Housing Act 1988 is very favourable to landlords compared to the previous legislation, and so there is now less incentive for granting a licence. A licence is simply a personal contract between two parties. A licence is most commonly created when the owner offers lodging, that is, the owner provides various services for the house sharer.

Where a person shares the owner's home with the owner, a licence may be created if the person sharing does not have exclusive possession of the house or part of it. The sharer will not have exclusive possession of parts of the house shared with the licensor, such as the kitchen or lounge. The licensor must actually use these common areas.

The licensee will not have exclusive possession of his own personal room if the licensor has a right to enter the room and actually exercises this right. Simply possessing a set of keys to the room is not sufficient. It is safe to say that if the licensor provides a service to the licensee that involves entering the room, there is no exclusive possession. Services such as bed-making, laundry, or cleaning involve regularly entering the room. Such a licensee is commonly called a lodger, and the licensor may also provide a breakfast or other meals.

The licensor should state or reserve the right to have unrestricted access to the room. For example, the licensor should not need to give the licensee notice that he will be entering the room, and the licensee must not be allowed to exclude the licensor from the room. In practice of course, it is sensible to have a routine time for providing the services, although you should be free to change the routine so that it is mutually convenient.

The licensee, then, will not have exclusive possession, but the licence will give the licensee the right personally to use that room and the licensor must respect that right and the licensee's privacy. The licensee should be allowed to enjoy using the room without interruption or interference by the licensor or others, and the room should be fit for the intended uses such as sleeping and studying.

The licence agreement should be drafted by a solicitor or qualified letting agent, and signed and dated by the licensor and licensee. It is important that the document is called a licence and not a lease and that the terms of the agreement are the sort of terms you would find in a licence and not in a lease. For example:

- the licence should not give the licensee 'exclusive possession' of his room;
- the words 'licence fee' should be used instead of 'rent';
- the licensor should 'grant the right' to use the property to the licensee, not 'let' or 'demise' it;
- as a licence is a personal contract, the agreement should state that the right to use the property is personal to the licensee;
- the licensor should not require the licensee to repair any part of the property, as repairing obligations are usual for leases only;
- however, the licensor can require the licensee to use the property in a good, proper and tidy manner.

The reason it is so important that the right terms and phrases are used and that the circumstances are actually those of a licence is that if a problem occurs, a court will examine the nature of the agreement and come to its own independent conclusion as to whether a lease or licence exists.

A licence can be a very flexible agreement, and can be for as short or long as the parties like. If the licence is for a fixed term, that is, it specifically states when it will begin and end, the parties should not break or revoke the licence before the term expires, unless they agree with each other that the licence may be revoked early. If either party does revoke the licence without agreement or unilaterally, that person will be in breach of contract. This would entitle the wronged party to claim monetary compensation. If there is a possibility that you might need to end the licence early, you should include a term known as a 'break clause' enabling you and/or the licensee to give notice and end the licence early.

Alternatively, the licence could be on a periodic basis such as weekly or monthly if the licence fee is paid weekly or monthly, which would continue indefinitely until either party gave advance warning or notice that he or she wished to end the licence. Usually the length of the warning period or notice is the same as the period of the licence, although in the case of a weekly licence, at least four weeks' notice should be given. Pages 98–99 cover terminating licences in more detail.

The licensor and licensee are free to agree what licence fee they like. The licence can also specify that the licence fee will be increased by a certain amount or percentage at a given date (or an unspecified amount to be agreed upon at the time, but this may well lead to arguments). The licence fee should take into account the services provided and anything else the licensee receives but does not pay for separately, such as electricity, gas and water. Your local newspaper should give you an idea of the going rates. A room or house that is well furnished or spacious, or convenient for the town centre or college, will command a higher licence fee than other places.

Leases

In other situations where you are not providing services to the sharer, it is safest to assume that the sharer will have exclusive possession of the room given to him for his own personal use. You should therefore grant the sharer a lease of the room with the right to use the shared rooms (the kitchen, lounge etc).

As long as you are actually living in the house as your only or main home and you personally grant the lease (that is, you do not grant the lease in the name of a company), the lease will be outside the Housing Act 1988 and the tenant will have no security of tenure or right to have the rent assessed. You must be living in the home when the lease is granted and you must continue to live there throughout the duration of the lease, otherwise the tenant will gain security of tenure and the lease will become an assured tenancy under the Act. Normal periods of absence, such as holidays and business trips, will not affect the status of the tenancy. If you are not the sole owner of the home and the lease is consequently granted to the tenant by you and one or more other people, only one of those people needs to be resident in the house or flat as his main home.

If you do need to leave your home, it is safest to terminate the lease or licence (see Chapter 9) and, if you so wish, create a new lease which should be in a similar form to a lease for an entire house or flat as discussed in Chapters 4 and 5.

Sensible rules for a peaceful life

As you will be living in close proximity to the licensee or tenant, it is a good idea to set up a system for the management of day-to-day household activities and expenses. Think about this aspect of sharing your home, and discuss it in advance with people interested in the room. Some of the rules that are fixed and definite can be included in the lease or licence. If the rules are then breached, it is possible in some circumstances to terminate the agreement (see Chapter 10), but the mere fact that the rules are set out in the agreement will serve to remind the licensee or tenant of his responsibilities.

Day-to-day running of the household
Try to imagine a typical day during the working week and at weekends, and how the household facilities will be shared.

Baths
The first thing you may want to do is have a bath or shower, and you do not want to find all the hot water has been used up, or your new house-mate is languishing in the bath for an hour. This may seem a small point, but little irritations can build up, and it may be worth having an informal agreement as to when baths are taken. If the bathroom is next to a bedroom, you might consider banning baths when the bedroom's occupant is asleep.

Security
Each person should be responsible for ensuring the house is properly locked up and all windows closed rather than leaving it to the last person to leave because it is easy to think that someone is in the house when in fact everyone has gone. In this way, security becomes a matter of habit and routine and is therefore less likely to be overlooked. There should also be a general rule that you let each other know if you intend to be away for a night or more. It is sensible to know where the person is in case there is an emergency, or it may transpire that you will both be away at the same time so you can arrange to cancel the milk and papers, turn off the timing system for heating and water, and make any other necessary arrangements.

Guests
Your house-mate will want to be able to invite friends back and cook for them at times, but he should also respect your peace and right to privacy, and vice versa. Try to talk about this issue when you show the prospective house-mate around, and do not choose

an extrovert socialite if you are a quiet bookworm yourself! You may wish to have a rule that all visitors should leave by 11 p.m.

More important is the decision as to whether you will allow your house-mate to have friends to stay the night. Besides your own personal views in the case of boyfriends or girlfriends, you should also think about the additional household expenses involved, such as hot water, and whether the house or flat is big enough to cope with an extra person. There are several options:

- completely prohibited;
- prohibited unless you decide on each occasion to permit it;
- permitted as long as specified conditions are met. For example you are given one or two days' advance warning; the guest is of the same/opposite sex; the guest stays in a specified room; the guest pays a contribution towards expenses; the guest stays only a specified number of nights per week or only on specified days of the week; the guest only stays when the licensee is present; no more than a specified number of guests may stay for any one night.
- freely permitted.

If the last option is chosen, you must be careful to ensure that an arrangement with one particular person is not so permanent or regular as to amount to an informal lease or licence to stay in the home.

If an individual guest does stay nearly all the time and you are happy for that to continue, you should consider discussing with your house-mate whether the current agreement should be terminated and a fresh agreement between you and both people jointly is drawn up. For this reason it is wise to specifically prohibit the house-mate from sub-letting his room or assigning it. Sub-letting occurs when a tenant in effect becomes a landlord himself to another person. A person is said to have assigned his lease when he permits another person to take his place as tenant. In the case of licences, the licence should be made personal to the licensee only, and he should be prohibited from taking in paying guests or lodgers. If you include these prohibitions, you should be entitled to ask your house-mate either to remedy the breach by telling the 'guest' to leave, or, if they fail to remedy the situation, you would be entitled to terminate the agreement.

Household bills

Unless there is a separate meter for the house-mate's own use, you will need to charge him for household bills or include a fixed amount in the licence fee or rent to cover the bills.

If you decide to charge separately, you could split the bill in proportion to the number of people in the house or flat, or you could charge the tenant or licensee the amount which is in excess of your usual bill. The latter is quite difficult to estimate and you will not be able to prove it was the house-mate who made the bill higher and not yourself in the event of a dispute.

Telephone bills are more difficult to deal with than gas, electricity or water rates as people vary greatly in how much they use the phone. You may decide that you do not want the house-mate to use the phone at all, or that only incoming calls may be received (before 11 p.m. and after 7 a.m. if you wish). If so, if you have an old-style dial telephone, it is worth buying a telephone lock from a hardware store to prevent unauthorised use (though be aware that these locks can sometimes be circumvented if you know how). If you only use the phone to receive calls rather than make them, it is possible for British Telecom or Mercury to make the phone 'one way' for a flat fee.

If you do allow the house-mate to use the phone, you could keep a log book of phone calls and work out how much each person uses on the basis of the number of units used. British Telecom will advise you about the price per unit. The rate varies according to the time of day and the area you are ringing. Some special code numbers, such as 0898 numbers, are very expensive to ring. Mercury use a different charging system based on the length of the call rather than the number of units used. The log book may look like this:

Date	Caller	Rate	Duration	Destination	Units used
1.9	Ann	Cheap	20 mins	London	4
2.9	Tom	Peak	2½ mins	Glasgow	3

It is possible to purchase a device that clicks over the number of units used which is more accurate than timing the call yourself.

Alternatively you could install a pay phone, or convert your own phone into a pay phone. However, it is quite expensive to do this, and phone calls from pay phones are more costly. You will, however, have the certainty of knowing that the house-mate must pay for each call as it is made.

For general household items such as cleaning fluids, light bulbs, toilet rolls etc., again you may decide to charge a flat rate incorporated in the licence fee or rent, or charge specifically. Such items can mount up, so it is worth giving this some thought. If you charge separately, keep a list on a notice board of the items and price that you or the house-mate have bought. Alternatively, you could have a 'kitty' or box into which you both put a certain amount of money each week, and items are bought with these funds. The problem with a kitty is that it is easy to lose track of who put in what, and it can be tempting to borrow money from it, or get the cash muddled with other money.

Cleaning rota
If you are taking in a lodger, cleaning services will usually be provided by you, and the lodger will only be responsible for their own personal tidiness. In other circumstances you should either divide the chores or take turns so that one person does not end up being burdened by all the 'nasty' jobs. Cleaning can be a major source of rows so it is important to establish a proper and fair routine, and to have a rule that all spills are cleared up instantly and washing up is not left undone. The licensee and tenant will be under a general duty to use the property in a good and proper manner, so if this does become a problem, you might have recourse to some remedies (see pages 107–9).

Your personal relationship with your house-mate

As you will be living in close proximity, you will probably get to know your house-mate quite well. The above rules will help this relationship so that neither party takes liberties and both respect each other's privacy. Even if you get to know your house-mate very well, it is still worth keeping to these rules, probably even more so as 'friends and business' do not mix easily and it can be very difficult trying to reassert rules. Although it is a good idea to be flexible about some issues and to adopt a general principle of live and let live, remember it is your home and you have the right to insist that the agreed rules are adhered to and your peace and privacy respected.

Equally, you should remember that your home is also in part your house-mate's home, and he should be made to feel independent and private too. Do not forget to take your repairing and maintenance responsibilities seriously (see pages 52-5), even though you might have let a problem go if you were not letting a room in your home.

If you choose a tenant or licensee wisely and keep to the rules you have agreed for the peace and comfort of you both, you have every chance that your relationship with your house-mate will be amicable and you will soon feel he is part of the family.

CHAPTER 4
Letting a whole house or flat: the theory

If you are intending to let a whole house or flat which you will not be living in yourself, the letting will probably be governed by the Housing Act 1988. This chapter will look at the effect of the Act and how it applies to a typical lease. Chapter 5 will look at some decisions that need to be made when letting a whole house or flat.

How the Housing Act 1988 affects you and your tenant

The Housing Act 1988 was introduced to revitalise the much needed private rented housing sector by abolishing some of the more restrictive rules, but also protecting the tenant from unfair practices. Generally, the Act will apply if the letting is to an individual person (that is, not a company) who uses the property as his main residential home. Lettings for business purposes do not come within the Act, nor do holiday lettings. The Act does not apply if the landlord resides in the property as his only or main residential home.

A word of warning. It is not possible to avoid the Act by reserving the option to reside in the property, or by labelling the letting a holiday let. A court would look at whether the landlord actually lived in the property, and the real purpose of the letting. Nor is it possible to contract out of the Act by agreeing with the tenant that it will not apply.

Under the Act there are two types of tenancy. You can decide which tenancy you prefer to create.

Assured tenancies and assured shorthold tenancies

Assured tenancies offer the tenant more protection than assured shorthold tenancies. If the landlord wants to end an assured tenancy, he must prove one of the special grounds listed in the Act (such as substantial rent arrears – see Chapter 9) to obtain an order for possession of the property. If the landlord wants to end an assured shorthold tenancy, as long as the duration of the lease has run its course, the landlord does not have to prove a special ground to obtain an order for possession, he just needs to show that the tenancy has come to an end and the proper notices have been given. The landlord of an assured shorthold tenancy can choose to prove a special ground if he wishes. If he wants to terminate the tenancy before the expiry of the term, he must prove a special ground.

An assured tenancy can be a fixed term of any length, or it can be a periodic lease (see page 20). An assured shorthold tenancy must be at least six months long, and the original or first term offered to the tenant must be fixed. But if an assured shorthold tenancy is renewed, the new lease can be periodic (see pages 97–8).

Statutory periodic tenancies

With both assured and assured shorthold tenancies, if the term of the lease runs out and the landlord has not obtained a possession order, the tenant is not an illegal occupant and does not have to leave. By statutory law a periodic tenancy comes into existence or is implied. This tenancy is known as a statutory periodic tenancy and the terms of the tenancy are the same as the old lease. As the new tenancy is periodic, it runs from one period to the next until it is brought to an end. The length of the period is determined by the frequency with which rent is paid (for example, if the rent is paid monthly, the statutory periodic tenancy will run from month to month).

Whether the old lease was an assured lease or an assured shorthold lease will affect the way in which the statutory periodic lease can be terminated. If the old lease was an assured lease, a ground must be proved to obtain a possession order. If the old lease was an assured shorthold lease, the landlord can prove a ground or just prove that the original lease came to an end and the proper notices have been given.

LETTING RESIDENTIAL PROPERTY

Rent
The other main difference between assured tenancies and assured shorthold tenancies is rent. Initially, there is more rent control for assured shorthold tenancies than for assured tenancies. During the original fixed term of the lease, the assured shorthold tenant can ask the Rent Assessment Committee to review the rent, whereas the assured tenant cannot. The Rent Assessment Committee is a panel of experts and lay people who consider the level of rents for their area. However, the Committee would only reduce the rent of an assured shorthold tenancy if it were significantly higher than the level of rent a landlord might reasonably be able to obtain. An assured shorthold rent is usually slightly lower than the rent for a comparable assured tenancy because the tenant does not have so much security of tenure.

Once the original fixed term of the assured shorthold tenancy comes to an end, if the landlord offers a new fixed term, the tenant has no right to go to the Committee. If the landlord simply allows a statutory periodic tenancy to arise and he raises the rent, the tenant can go to the Committee. By contrast, an assured tenant can go to the Committee whether a new fixed term is offered or a statutory periodic tenancy arises. Rents and rent reviews are considered in more detail on pages 72–3 and 79–83.

Which type of tenancy should you choose?
Strictly speaking, you should offer an assured tenancy for long leases of, say, five years or more, and an assured shorthold tenancy for short leases. In practice, though, many landlords create assured shorthold tenancies in preference to assured tenancies even though they are happy for the tenant to stay in the property for some time. This is because, although there is a minimum length of lease that must be created for assured shorthold tenancies (six months) there is no maximum. Despite the fact that there is initially more rent control for assured shorthold tenancies, assured shorthold tenancies seem to appeal to landlords firstly because they have an immediate right to recover the property at the end of the term without having to prove a ground, and secondly because after the original term has expired and a new fixed term has begun, there is no rent control. A landlord can then 'get the best of both worlds' by having a long-term stay tenant but little rent control.

The landlord could create a lease for the minimum length of time for assured shorthold tenancies, and when the six months is up, a further lease of six months could be entered into, and further six month leases after that for as long as the parties are happy that the arrangement should continue. Alternatively, the landlord could grant the minimum term lease of six months, and then allow the tenant to stay on under a statutory periodic tenancy. The advantage of this is that a new lease need not be written as the terms will be the same as the old lease. The disadvantage is that a tenant who has a statutory periodic tenancy can apply to the Rent Assessment Committee for rent review. However, if the tenant indicated that he wanted to apply for a rent review, the landlord could always resort to terminating the tenancy. It is, of course, always better to come to an amicable agreement rather than resort to the Rent Assessment Committee or threaten to terminate the lease.

The type of tenancy you create will also depend on what sort of tenancy the tenant is prepared to accept. A student or someone who is thinking he might move to a different area soon might be quite happy to accept the relatively insecure methods above, but others may be looking to settle down for some while, and might insist on an assured tenancy, or a long assured shorthold tenancy. This will be a matter for negotiation, and will depend on whether you want a long-term stay tenant, and how keen you are on the particular tenant interested in the property.

Although the Act does regulate tenancies and offers tenants protection from having their leases terminated suddenly without notice or unfairly, it is in fact easy enough to follow these regulations. No landlord will have to put up with a problem tenant either. If the tenant is breaching covenants, not paying due rent, mistreating the furniture etc, the landlord can terminate the lease under the provisions of the Act – Chapter 10 deals with these issues.

The following are some simple examples illustrating the differences between assured tenancies and assured shorthold tenancies.

Example of an assured tenancy

Leo grants Tom a three-year assured tenancy. Tom is not happy with the rent as there are several other lettings in the area which are considerably cheaper. He cannot apply to the Rent Assessment Committee; even if the lease provides that the rent will be increased further, he still cannot do anything about it.

At the end of the lease, Leo wants Tom to leave. Tom does

not agree to go of his own accord, so Leo must prove a special ground to the court to obtain an order for possession.

Alternatively, at the end of the three years, Leo is happy for Tom to stay on. Whether Tom stays under a statutory periodic tenancy or under a new lease, Tom can go to the Rent Assessment Committee.

Leo wants Tom to leave at the end of the statutory periodic tenancy. As Tom does not agree to go of his own accord, he has a right to stay there until Leo proves a special ground and obtains an order for possession.

Example of an assured shorthold tenancy

Larry gives Tim a six-month assured shorthold tenancy. Tim is not happy with the rent, so he can go to the Rent Assessment Committee during the initial six-month period.

At the end of the six-month lease, Larry wants Tim to leave. Larry does not need to prove a special ground if he needs to obtain an order for possession from the court.

Alternatively, at the end of the six months, Larry agrees that Tim may stay. If he stays on under a statutory periodic tenancy, Tim can resort to the Rent Assessment Committee, but if a new lease is granted, Tim cannot go to the Committee.

At the end of the new lease or statutory periodic tenancy, Larry wants Tim to leave. As Tim does not agree to go of his own accord, Larry can get an order for possession without needing to prove a special ground.

What happens if the tenant wants to leave?

As the lease is a contract, the tenant is obliged to stay for the full term. However, a 'break clause' can be written into the agreement which gives the landlord and/or the tenant the opportunity of ending the lease early if either so wishes. For assured shorthold tenancies, the break clause must not be operable within the first six months of the term. If a landlord and tenant cannot agree that the break clause be used if it is the landlord wanting to end the lease early, the landlord must go to court and ask for the lease to be terminated. This is because a landlord cannot end a tenancy under the Housing Act earlier than the expiry of the term if the tenant does not agree. The landlord cannot get around the Act by writing things into the lease which enable him to terminate the lease in a manner not allowed by the Act. The tenant, however, can give due notice according to a break clause and terminate the lease if that is what they originally agreed, and he does not need to seek the landlord's agreement again. Once a tenant terminates the lease, he loses protection under the Housing Act.

How to create an assured tenancy

If you have decided to create an assured tenancy you need not actually do anything to make it an assured tenancy. The tenancy will automatically be an assured tenancy if the Act applies (see pages 38-9) and if the landlord has not opted to create an assured shorthold tenancy. It is a good idea, however, to describe the lease as an assured tenancy under the Housing Act 1988 for the sake of clarity and certainty.

How to create an assured shorthold tenancy

To create an assured shorthold tenancy you must give the tenant a notice of an assured shorthold tenancy. <u>The notice must be given to the tenant and signed by the landlord and tenant at least a week before the tenancy begins, and you must not back-date the notice, even if the tenant agrees to back-dating. If the notice is not properly given, the tenancy will be an assured tenancy instead of an assured shorthold tenancy by law. Specially printed notices can be obtained from stationers. Your solicitor or letting agent should provide you with a notice.</u>

The notice is simple to complete. <u>The notice tells the tenant that the tenancy is to be an assured shorthold tenancy and about his rights in brief. All you and the tenant have to do is fill in the blanks for the names of the parties, the address of the tenanted property and the length of the tenancy. The notice should be kept in a safe place. It is a good idea to include in the lease a clause acknowledging when the notice was given and that the lease is an assured shorthold tenancy.</u> Things to note about creating an assured shorthold tenancy:

- You can only create an assured shorthold tenancy if the length

of the lease is fixed and definite; the original lease (as compared to renewals) cannot be periodic.
- The length of the lease must be at least six months.
- You cannot create an assured shorthold tenancy if the tenant has lived in the house or flat previously as a tenant under an assured tenancy. The new lease must be another assured tenancy unless the tenant agrees otherwise. There is an exception to this. If you are a new landlord, that is, a different, previous landlord gave the tenant the assured tenancy, you can offer the tenant an assured shorthold tenancy when the assured tenancy comes to an end.

Letting your own home

If the house or flat you wish to let is your main residential home and you intend to live there again in the future, you will want to ensure that you can recover possession of the property easily. Probably the best type of tenancy to offer is an assured shorthold tenancy because, as we have seen, at the end of the term you are absolutely entitled to the recovery of the property without having to prove a ground. However, you may wish to completely exclude the possibility of the tenant referring the rent to the Rent Assessment Committee, or you might not be able to offer the minimum six months' term required of an assured shorthold tenancy. You may instead need to create an assured tenancy, either periodic or fixed.

A landlord who lets his own home during his absence by creating an assured tenancy comes under a special rule in the Housing Act. The landlord can be absolutely sure of gaining possession if the landlord gives notice of the fact that the landlord might want to recover possession because the property is the landlord's main residence. The legal jargon for this notice is 'Ground 1 Notice' because it is the first of the grounds for possession under the Act.

Your solicitor or letting agent will help you to draft the notice which should be given to the tenant no later than the day the tenancy begins. The notice should state that the landlord might seek possession under this ground and that, prior to the tenancy, the landlord occupied the property as his principal residence. The ground also covers the case where the landlord (or his spouse) simply requires the property as their dwelling house. So, for example, if you were abroad and decided on your return not to live in your house but to sell it instead, you could still gain possession. Refer to Chapter 9 for more information about terminating tenancies.

The following chapters will deal with the 'life cycle' of the assured tenancy and the assured shorthold tenancy – changing the rent, renewing the lease, changing the terms, ending the lease. But first, at the planning stages, there are still a number of practical decisions you need to make about how to organise the letting.

CHAPTER 5
Letting a whole house or flat: the practice

A whole house or flat can be let in a variety of ways:

- by a lease to one person;
- by a lease to several people all together;
- by several leases (or possibly licences) to several people individually.

How you let the property will depend on:

- the suitability of the property for the type of letting;
- how much rent you need to collect;
- personal preferences for individual or group lettings.

Suitability of the property for the type of letting

This may be fairly obvious: for example, the property might obviously be only big enough for a bachelor flat or married couple, but take a good look around the property and see whether a few simple adjustments could give you more options. A study or living room could be changed into an extra bedroom, a partition could create an extra room, or if you are prepared to spend some more money on adjustments, an extension could be built on, or the attic converted into a bedroom. If the property is comprised of several bedrooms plus living accommodation, you can choose to let to one person, or to a group of people jointly, or to several people separately.

Overcrowding

If you are letting the property to a number of people you must not overcrowd it. Besides being a criminal offence, it could also lead to problems running the household. A general guide is that if two or more people of the opposite sex, who are not married to each other or living together as husband and wife, have to sleep in the same room, the property is overcrowded. Children over the age of nine should not have to share a room with someone of the opposite sex. The property should also have adequate toilet facilities for the number of people in the house.

Rent

It is not necessarily the case that the more tenants you have the more rent you can collect. The level of rent will depend on the state of the property and its amenities. For example, you might be able to attract an individual or couple to a spacious property but collect the same amount of rent as if you had let every room to individuals, as long as the property is nice enough to attract the sort of people who could afford a high rent. On the other hand, if the property is rather basic but large, you might find it difficult to attract a single person or couple for the level of rent you need to set in order to make the letting profitable. It may be better to let the rooms separately so that each room has an affordable rent, but the house as a whole is let for a profitable sum when all the rents are added together.

Personal preferences for individual or group lettings

Some people prefer to let their property to a single person or just a couple because they feel 'safer' and that the arrangement is more 'manageable' as there are fewer people to deal with. Of course, this will depend on the sort of individual or couple you choose, but it is probably true to say that a couple or mature single person is more likely to be settled and responsible than, say, a group of young students. This may be an important consideration if the property has valuable furniture in it. It is, however, perfectly possible to choose reliable groups of people by following the guidelines set out in Chapter 8.

Letting to a group of people

There are two ways of letting to groups:

- by one lease to a group of people all together;
- or by several leases (or licences) to several people separately.

In many ways the first arrangement is easier. The tenants will have what is known as joint and several liability. This means that they are not only responsible for themselves individually, they are also responsible for each other. All the tenants are liable for the entire rent of the property. Individually they may come to some private arrangement as to the sharing of the rent, but legally you can pursue any or all of them for the whole rent, not just 'their share' of it. This is particularly useful if one tenant 'disappears' for some reason. Also, if one tenant, for example, breaks something, all the tenants are responsible for repairing it. Tenants in this situation are more likely to pull together and organise the running of the household well, as their joint and several liability gives them an incentive to do this.

To let the property as a whole under one agreement, all the parties to the agreement must sign and date it at the same time, and they must all share the same property for the same length of time. The tenants are likely to be related to each other in some way as they will need to form a group before they look to rent a property. They may, for example, be husband and wife, or friends who know each other from work or college. If you want to let the property as a whole, the property should be in a suitable condition to attract tenants who know each other. A group of friends, for example, will probably require a sitting room for socialising whereas this would not be so important for strangers renting rooms separately. A husband and wife and possibly family will want to make a home for themselves, and will be looking for a nicely furnished place rather than a cheap place more attractive to students with little money.

If the property is to be under multiple occupation, that is, let to individuals separately, each person will be responsible for his actions only, and for the rent or licence fee which he has individually agreed with you.

The advantage of letting a house to individuals is that, as each person has a separate agreement, individuals may live in the property for different lengths of time. Whereas under a single agreement the need for one person to leave may cause the entire household to terminate their agreement, in a multiple letting there can be a rolling stock of occupiers – one person leaves to be replaced by another. You will receive less money for the period during which that room is unoccupied, but it is unlikely that the whole house or flat will be unoccupied for periods at a time as with single lets to a group.

Usually the multiply-occupied house or flat suits young single people who like to have the freedom to move about easily. Their requirements are usually more basic and simple than those looking for a single letting, and there need not necessarily be a living room. Your expenditure on the furnishing of the property may be less, but the level of rent or licence fee will reflect this.

As each individual occupier makes a separate agreement with you, you are free to choose the person who moves into the vacant room. For the sake of household harmony it is sensible to allow the existing tenants to meet the prospective house-mate and have some say as to who moves in, as you do not want the occupiers to clash with each other and not co-operate in the running of the house, or, worse still, move out. It is a good idea to impose general household rules in the agreement, such as regarding the taking of baths, and to set up a system of sharing household expenses and dealing with other household concerns as discussed on pages 32–6 on letting a room in your own home.

In general, you or your agent will need to keep a closer eye on multiple occupations than on single lets to ensure that the occupiers are co-operating with each other and that the property is in a good state of repair. It is important that neighbours are not offended by the nature of the occupation, so if, for example, knowing the occupiers you think they are unlikely to tend the garden, you might consider it wise to employ a gardener or to do it yourself, and allow for this expense when you set the rent. You should also consider imposing the following conditions in the agreement in particular: not to keep any animals; and not to play any musical instrument, television or record player at anti-social hours. These and other conditions are considered in detail in Chapter 6.

Lease or licence?

If you decide to let the property as a whole to an individual or a group, you should create a lease. This is because the tenants will have the right of exclusive possession – they will have the right to exclude other people from the property. You cannot enter the property (unless you are inspecting it or making repairs as explained on page 54) and neither can you allow other people to enter the property or live there. The tenants will have one agreement, share the same title (that is, leasehold) for the same length of time, so all the conditions of creating a lease rather than a licence are met.

Multiple occupations may be either a lease or a licence depending upon the circumstances. As explained on page 24, there is a danger that, although you may try to create a licence, the law might decide that, in reality, a lease exists. For example, it is highly likely that the courts would consider the true nature of the agreement is a lease if all the occupiers move in at the same time, choose for themselves which room will be their own so that in effect they all have combined exclusive possession, and their agreements are similar and all end on the same date.

To avoid such disputes and uncertainties it is usually sensible to create a lease to the individuals when you are letting a house or flat which you do not live in. This is because, if an occupier successfully proves that a lease exists instead of a licence, the occupier will gain an assured tenancy whereas you may have preferred to have created an assured shorthold tenancy.

How long should the lease be?

The first consideration will be practicality and convenience: how long is the property available for letting, and when do you need possession of the property? If it is difficult to ascertain this, you might be advised to consider creating an assured periodic lease, or a minimum six-month assured shorthold lease followed by either an express periodic lease, or a statutory periodic tenancy, so that the lease can be ended quickly if necessary.

The law is different in some respects according to the length of the lease. Basically, the most important distinctions are as follows:

- If the lease is for less than seven years (or the landlord can end the lease within seven years) the landlord has greater responsibilities for repair and maintenance than if the lease were for more than seven years.
- If the lease is for 21 years or more it is called a 'long lease'. The tenant can register his interest at the Land Registry, and may

have special rights of security of tenure under the Landlord and Tenant Act 1954. In some circumstances the tenant may be eligible for 'leasehold enfranchisement' which is ending the lease by buying the freehold from the landlord and becoming the outright owner. Usually, instead of rent being payable at regular intervals, the tenant pays an initial sum or premium, and then a nominal or small 'ground rent' each year. For these reasons long leases are not considered in detail in this book.

CHAPTER 6
Responsibilities of landlord and tenant and licensor and licensee

The commonest cause of dispute between landlords and tenants, and licensors and licensees, is usually over their respective obligations; it can ruin the relationship between them and lead to early termination of the lease or not renewing it when it runs out. If matters are serious, one or other might take the case to court with all the time and expense that that entails. The best way to avoid disputes is to set out the obligations clearly and precisely in the lease so that there are no 'grey areas' to argue about.

These obligations will be expressed as covenants or terms in the lease or licence. If the covenant or term is breached or broken, the injured party can go to court and make the other party keep the covenant, or seek a termination of the lease or licence and/or seek money or damages as compensation.

Maintenance and repair
This is often the biggest area for disputes.

The tenant's obligation is to use the property in a tenant-like manner, and a similar obligation is imposed on a licensee. This means the occupier should use the property and its contents carefully and properly as one would expect someone to use their own home. He should repair anything that he or his guests damage. He should not destroy or remove anything – for example, he should not get rid of the sofa or fell a tree. All these things are implied by law, but it is worth mentioning them specifically in the lease.

What the landlord should do
The tenant's obligations usually relate to the interior of the house and the landlord's obligations to the exterior. If the lease is for less than seven years, or if the landlord can terminate the lease within seven years because he has put a clause in the lease giving himself that option, any covenant by the tenant to repair the structure and exterior of the property is void. By law (the Landlord and Tenant Act 1985) the landlord of such a tenancy must:

- repair the structure and exterior of the property (such as the drains and gutters);
- keep supply services in working order (ensure the bath, sink and toilet work, the gas, electricity and water are on and safe and that the immersion heater works);
- keep the installations in the house in working order (for example, the gas fire, kettle and vacuum cleaner if these are provided by the landlord).

In addition, if the tenancy is an assured tenancy or an assured shorthold tenancy the landlord must repair anything that affects the ability of the tenant to use the property, even if the thing that needs repairing is not specifically included as part of the letting in the lease. So, for example, the landlord could not get out of repairing the roof by excluding it from the lease.

Repairing the roof and other parts of the structure and exterior of the house or flat can be very expensive. For leases under seven years the landlord cannot make the tenant agree in the lease that he will pay for such repairs, as by law that covenant would be unenforceable. For leases over seven years, the landlord and tenant can come to their own arrangement about these kinds of repair and the landlord can also ask for money for the repairs or for money on account of the repairs (see Service Charges on pages 63-7). However, if the lease gave the tenant onerous covenants, such as repairing the roof, the tenant could rightly negotiate a low rent.

What the tenant should do
With other types of repair, the landlord can make the tenant carry out the duty, whatever the length of the lease. The landlord can make the tenant repair anything that needs repairing because the tenant has failed to use it in a tenant-like manner (for example, if the tenant threw a ball through the window rather than the window cracking due to old age or a strong wind).

The tenant is responsible for repairing anything the tenant is entitled to remove from the property. As we have seen, the tenant should not remove anything from the house or flat, but if an item is an exception to this, the landlord does not have to repair it. The tenant must repair his own vacuum cleaner, for example, but the landlord should repair it if it forms part of the property.

Incidentally, if an 'Act of God' occurs, the landlord does not have to repair the property – so if a river floods the house the lease terminates. The landlord should insure against 'Acts of God'.

When the repairs should be made

A landlord is only obliged to make a repair once he has received notice from the tenant that the repair needs to be made, or once he has inspected the property and found that the repair needs to be made. The lease should state that the tenant must notify the landlord promptly of any repairs needed. It should also permit the landlord and others (such as workmen) to enter and inspect the property. The Housing Act 1988 implies a term into the lease that the tenant should allow the landlord reasonable access to carry out the repairs but it is sensible to make this an express term to be sure that the tenant is aware of this obligation. It is important that things needing repair are not left to deteriorate further, as the resulting damage could become far worse than the original problem. These clauses are therefore very important.

The landlord is only obliged to make the repairs within a 'reasonable time'. What is reasonable will depend on the type of repair and how urgent it is. To prevent disputes, the lease could provide a time limit within which repairs must be made, for example, one month.

The lease should also state that the tenant should make the repairs he is obliged to carry out promptly, and that following inspection of the property, the landlord can give the tenant notice that the tenant must repair a list of things that the tenant is responsible for.

Standard of repair

Repair does not mean renew or improve, so a landlord does not need to put a new roof on if the roof leaks, or replace an ordinary cooker with a more sophisticated one. The repair need only be in keeping with the character and age of the property, so for example, basic student accommodation need not be upgraded, nor an old house modernised. However, the landlord must not use the age or character of the house to excuse not doing necessary repairs.

Wear and tear

Usually a lease obliges the tenant to return the property or 'yield up' the property in the same condition it was in at the start of the lease. In short leases, say those under seven years, it is common for 'reasonable wear and tear' to be excepted, and a tenant will probably expect this exception. The exception will mean, for example, that the tenant need not repair worn out linen, carpets or furniture or a chair that breaks because of old age. The wear and tear is reasonable if the item has been used properly and for its ordinary purpose – a chair broken because it was used as a step stool, or a table scratched as a result of mending a bike on it is not reasonable wear and tear.

Decorating

It is usual to prohibit decorating by the tenant in short leases or in any lease if the landlord prefers to do it himself. In longer leases the landlord may be happy for the tenant to do his own decorating. To ensure the tenant keeps the property in a good state of decoration, the lease may state that decorating must be done every three years. The landlord should make external decorations.

Alterations

It is unlikely that a landlord would want the tenant to alter the property in any way such as knocking down walls and erecting aerials, especially if the lease is short. With assured tenancies and assured shorthold tenancies, the lease can either completely prohibit the alterations, or prohibit them unless the landlord consents to the alterations. It is generally best that the landlord retains full control over any alterations or improvements as they may affect the value of the property.

Assignment and sub-letting

Assignment is where a tenant in effect gives away his lease to another person who steps into the tenant's shoes. The new person or 'assignee' becomes the tenant of the original landlord.

If the lease does not specifically prohibit assignment, the tenant is entitled to assign his lease. The landlord could then end up with an undesirable tenant whom he has not chosen. The landlord of an assured tenancy or an assured shorthold tenancy may absolutely prohibit assignment, or he may permit it if the tenant first obtains the landlord's consent.

Sub-letting is where the tenant remains the tenant but lets the property, or part of it, to someone else, the 'sub-tenant'. There are now two tenants, the original tenant, and the sub-tenant (also known as a sub-lessee). There are also two landlords. The original tenant becomes the landlord of the new sub-tenant. Again, in this situation the landlord could end up with a problem tenant as he will not have chosen the new sub-tenant.

It is often difficult and complicated for a landlord to enforce the obligations under the lease when the property has been assigned or sub-let. In some cases, the landlord can only make the original tenant carry out the obligations in the hope that the original tenant will make the new tenant perform the obligations for him. This is very difficult if the original tenant is hard to contact. The new tenant could also acquire rights of possession against the original landlord which the landlord might not desire.

Assignment and sub-letting is a very large and complex area of the law which is beyond the scope of a book of this nature. The decision whether or not to permit assignment and sub-letting very much depends on the type of lease and the type of property in question, but it is suggested that for short leases under seven years assignment and sub-letting is not advisable. The tenant of a short lease should not be able to insist on this right as most landlords of short leases refuse to grant it, and so he could not argue that the landlord was being unreasonable. Instead of assignment or sub-letting it is preferable that the lease is terminated or surrendered and a new lease made directly between the landlord and the new tenant (see Chapter 9). The original tenant might introduce the new tenant to the landlord (and indeed it could be the landlord's condition that he will only accept early termination of the lease if the tenant finds a new tenant), but the landlord will make all the proper checks and investigations of the new tenant's credentials and remain in full control of the situation.

The lease should also prohibit the tenant from parting with possession of the property or allowing another person to share the property with him.

Use of the property

To be an assured tenancy or an assured shorthold tenancy, the property must be used as the residential home of the tenant. Business tenancies have different rights of security of tenure and you do not want to have a business tenancy by accident. Another reason why you should insist in the lease that the property is used only for residential purposes is because all properties are classified for planning purposes as being for different uses, such as residential or business or trade, and you cannot change from one category of use to another without obtaining permission from the planning authorities. The reason for this is to prevent, say, a fish and chip shop from being set up in a quiet residential street and causing a nuisance.

Leases should also prohibit the tenant from using the property for an illegal or immoral purpose as there is no general or implied covenant to this effect.

Being a nuisance or annoyance to others

Although it might be possible for a landlord or other person to bring an action in court (under the law of tort), to prevent a nuisance it is much easier to specifically prohibit the tenant from being a nuisance or annoyance. This then gives the landlord the right to end the lease in some circumstances if the tenant does create a nuisance, thus solving the problem swiftly. The clause should state that the tenant should not do anything that may be a nuisance or annoyance in the opinion of the landlord so that the landlord is the arbiter of what is good behaviour. The lease may have this general clause only, or it may be more specific such as prohibiting the tenant from playing loud music, hanging items out of the window, or keeping pets. If the property is part of a group of flats, or is a room in a house, the covenants may be more specific still, such as not to play music, take baths or make telephone calls between the hours of, say, 11 pm and 7 am.

Fitness for habitation

If the property is furnished by the landlord there is a covenant in the lease implied by law that the property is fit for human habitation. The landlord may exclude this covenant in the lease by stating that the landlord makes no such covenant. For licences there may be implied terms for fitness, safety and suitability of the property. Liability for death or personal injury which results from the licensor's negligence cannot be excluded by the licensor, but liability for damage to personal property can be excluded.

Provision of fire escapes and equipment

Special rules about fire escapes apply to flats and conversions of houses into flats. Generally these rules only apply to large multiply-occupied houses which are at least three storeys high, but the local authority can inspect all multiply-occupied houses or flats and specify fire regulations. The rules are based on common sense, and all landlords and licensors should observe them in any case. The house or flat should have:

- Adequate means of escape from fire. This may mean providing a special fire escape staircase on the outside of the building and extra doors providing access to the outside in different parts of the house or flat. A balance must be maintained between security measures such as double-locking doors and barring and bolting windows and means of escape. Escape routes should be clearly identified and illuminated by special lighting because smoke obscures vision and disorientates people. Prominent notices explaining what to do in the event of fire and escape routes should be displayed.
- Adequate means of detecting fire. Smoke detectors are essential as they alert occupants to the presence of fire before smoke overcomes them, and they provide valuable extra time for escape. Several smoke detectors should be placed at strategic points in every room and hall ways, and they should be tested regularly.
- Adequate means of fighting fire. Plenty of fire extinguishers, fire blankets, and fire sand should be placed at strategic points throughout the house or flat. If it is considered necessary, a sprinkler system should be installed. These systems detect smoke and automatically sprinkle water. A closed door will keep fire contained in one room for valuable minutes before it spreads, so doors should be thick and fireproofed.

If a local authority considers that there is a serious risk of fire in a building, it has the power to apply for a closing order from a Magistrates Court. This order takes effect as soon as it is granted and the building must be evacuated and no one will be permitted to occupy it until proper facilities are installed.

Furniture

Although the tenant is not allowed by law to remove furniture from the property, there is nothing to stop him from moving the furniture from one room to another. If the property is your own home, it would obviously be a great inconvenience to find that, say, the sitting room had been turned into a bedroom. At the end of the tenant's stay it would also be quite troublesome to have to put the furniture back in place ready for the next tenant. You might therefore consider putting a clause in the lease to say that the furniture must either not be moved, or that, at the end of the term, the furniture must be left in the same place as it was originally found at the commencement of the term.

Bills

Under the old rates system the landlord paid the rates as this was a tax on the property which was owned by the landlord. The council tax is a personal tax, and is therefore usually the responsibility of the tenant. Some exceptions are made for property let to students and property in multiple occupation. Your local council will advise you in detail about this. If the property is left standing empty, the landlord will usually be liable for a charge.

Services such as gas, electricity, telephone and water are for the tenant's own personal use and should be paid by him. To ensure this, see that the bills are in the name of the tenant or one or more of the joint tenants, and not in the landlord's name.

Alternatively, the landlord may describe the rent as all-inclusive of these bills and raise the rent accordingly, or pay the bill and ask for the money from the tenant. This may be convenient if you are letting a room in your own home (see Chapter 3), but otherwise it can lead to problems. The tenant might leave without paying the bills, or you might forget to ask to be reimbursed, or the bill could arrive long after the tenant has left, or, if the rent is inclusive of bills, the tenant might be very wasteful and the inclusive amount may not be sufficient. These problems, obviously, will not occur if these services are paid for through a slot meter.

Why these terms and conditions are useful

The purpose of putting clauses like the ones discussed above in a lease is threefold:

- to divide the responsibilities and obligations of running the house or flat clearly and fairly between the landlord and tenant so that there is no room for argument;
- to remind the landlord and tenant of their responsibilities and obligations;
- to enable the landlord or tenant to have a remedy for breach of these covenants (see Chapter 10). Often the threat of action is sufficient.

How many covenants and the nature of the covenants you include in the lease is up to you and your solicitor or letting agent. However, you should bear in mind that a long lease full of 'thou shalt nots' is very off-putting to a prospective tenant, especially if the tenant's obligations run to pages whereas the landlord's are only a couple of lines. Also, some covenants, such as 'the tenant shall wash the windows each month/vacuum clean the carpets each week' may be impractical for the landlord to enforce, and should be best left to the tenant's duty to use the property in a tenant-like manner. However, it may be sensible to refer expressly to some matters if they cause you particular concern and you would like to draw them to the tenant's attention. Terms can also be stated in an attempt to impose some general 'house rules', but again, it may be difficult to actually enforce them. The following is a list of common prohibitions:

- not to use candles, paraffin or oil heaters, or keep any combustible goods on the property;
- not to hang clothes or other articles on the outside of the property;
- not to keep any animals;
- not to play any musical instrument or any television, radio or music system at unsocial hours/between the hours of, for example, 10 pm and 9 am;

- not to cause or permit damage to the property or the landlord's fixtures or fittings, and to preserve the property from loss, destruction or damage and not to remove any part from the property and to yield up the furniture in the same position, state and condition as at the start of the term;
- not to place any article on or obstruct in any way those parts of the building used in common with other occupiers;
- to inform the landlord if the tenant intends to be absent from the property for more than, say, 21 days;
- to turn off the water and drain the pipes if the tenant is absent from the property for more than 24 hours;
- to put the dustbin bags out for collection each week by the dustmen no earlier than 12 hours before collection.

CHAPTER 7
Letting a block of flats or a conversion

Letting a block of flats or a conversion (a house converted into separate flats) is much more involved than letting a separate dwelling house or rooms in a house. If you are not experienced in this field it would be sensible to appoint a professional manager to oversee the running of the flats. It is essential to obtain good legal advice which is relevant to the particular block or conversion you want to let.

Planning the letting

There are a number of important matters you will need to discuss with your solicitor, so it is worth giving them some initial consideration yourself first.

1. *How long should the leases be?*
   Is it important that the leases should all expire on the same day? Consider the different responsibilities for different lease periods (pages 50–51).

2. *What sort of tenancy?*
   Refer to Chapter 4 to consider differences between assured tenancies and assured shorthold tenancies.

3. *Is a plan necessary?*
   As parts of the building will be shared by others it is very important that the lease defines the extent of the let property clearly and precisely. If the let areas are difficult to define, a

LETTING A BLOCK OF FLATS OR A CONVERSION

plan may assist. Depending on the size of the building the plan may be only a rough guide, or an accurate, scaled plan drawn up by a surveyor.

4. *What access will the tenants need?*
   The lease will need to provide easements – for example, the right to use a staircase not forming part of the let property in order to gain access to a first floor flat, or the right to drive over part of another tenant's driveway to park a car in a garage. Other rights may be provided, such as the right to use the garden in common with the other tenants.

5. *How will the property be made secure both from other tenants and from outsiders?*
   Will it be necessary to employ a security man, or install an intercom?

6. *What means of escape are there in the event of fire?*
   The lease should detail escape routes in the event of fire. Special rules and regulations apply to many flats and conversions. Refer to page 58–9 for the landlord's responsibilities regarding the provisions of adequate means of preventing, fighting, and escaping from fire.

7. *How will the tenants dispose of household waste?*
   Communal bins and access to them will need to be provided.

8. *Are there to be parking facilities?*
   Is parking on-street, or are there spaces provided within the property? To allow for flexibility in the case of changes in tenants or renovations to the buildings, it is usual to grant just a right to park a certain number of cars in a specified parking area rather than include a particular parking space as part of the let property.

Service charges

The communal areas will need looking after. As all tenants use the areas, it is not fair to make one tenant responsible. It would not be practicable to make every tenant responsible as each one might expect the others to do the work. As you will still have rights over the communal areas if you have not granted them to any of the tenants, you will need to see that they are kept in a good state of repair so that they do not become a liability or cause an accident. It is therefore easier to undertake to maintain the areas (in practice, you might employ a handyman to do this for you). For leases of over seven years long, you can recoup the expenditure by levying a service charge on the tenants.

What to charge for
The service charge may include:

- maintenance, cleaning, repair and redecoration of communal areas;
- gas and electricity for the areas;
- employing a door man or security staff;
- employing a gardener;
- gas, electricity and water rates and maintenance and other running costs of a boiler, which serves all flats (that is, where the flats do not each have separate supplies);
- insurance;
- anything else that the landlord considers reasonably necessary.

How much to charge
The Landlord and Tenant Act 1985 states that the costs taken into account when deciding how much service charge should be payable should be reasonably incurred, and the services or the work must be of a reasonable standard. A tenant could therefore challenge the level of service charge if the work was unnecessary, badly done or overpriced. If costs exceed certain limits more detailed rules apply. Currently, tenants must be consulted about any work that is going to cost more than £1000 or more than £50 multiplied by the number of flats, whichever is the greater. If the tenants are not consulted they will only be obliged to pay £50 each or £1000 divided by the number of flats, whichever is the greater, unless the work was particularly urgent or the court says that the landlord acted reasonably in the circumstances. In some cases, at least two estimates for the work must be obtained and a notice and copy of the estimates must be given to the tenants who are allowed to make observations and comments about the work and price. The landlord must take these comments and observations into account.

Who to charge
If the flats are the same size and therefore enjoy the same services and supplies equally, it is simplest to divide the service charge

LETTING A BLOCK OF FLATS OR A CONVERSION

equally between them all. This should be stated clearly in the leases so there is no room for argument. If the flats are different sizes, you might consider apportioning the charges so that the tenants of the largest flats pay proportionately more than tenants of smaller flats. Apportioning can be done by setting a service charge at £x per square foot or metre, and then by measuring the floor spaces of the flats. This can be tedious and time consuming, so you might prefer to ask the tenants to pay fractions of the service charge, for example one pays a quarter, another a half and another a quarter. This should be stated in the lease.

When to charge

As it would not make sense commercially to pay for the work first and then recoup the cost from the tenants, you will probably want to charge in advance. There are various ways of charging in advance:

1. One lump sum specified in the lease at the beginning of each year. At the end of the year, an adjustment is made and either money claimed from the tenant, or any excess returned.

    This method can cause problems if there is a large expense early in the year but the extra money needed can only be claimed at the end of the year.

    If the lease is for longer than one or two years, there should be a provision entitling the landlord to increase the advance sum.

2. Two lump sums at six-month intervals with adjustments every six months.

    This is a slightly better method than 1 as the adjustments can be made more frequently. It is relatively inflexible, but may suit small flats where the landlord is reasonably sure of what the expenses will be.

3. Either method 1 or 2, but instead of specifying a sum in the lease, the lease states that a percentage of last year's service charge is payable at specified intervals.

    This method is only possible if there was a previous service charge. It might be more accurate than specifying a lump sum but there may still be unforeseen large expenses such as roof repairs.

4. Stating in the lease that a service charge shall be payable at such level and at such times as the landlord thinks reasonable.

This method would be ideal as it offers the landlord maximum flexibility. However, it could be difficult to get the tenant's agreement to it. The tenant might be more willing to agree if the lease states some limits, such as that each service charge demand will not be more than a specified amount and will not be demanded more than a certain number of times per year. Again, the lease should provide for an adjustment of the charge.

Service charge accounts must be given to the tenant promptly. Besides being good management, if the account is for costs incurred more than 18 months ago, the tenant can refuse to pay that amount.

Rights of tenants
If the service charge is variable (instead of a specified sum fixed by the lease), the tenant is able to make the following enquiries to which the landlord must respond:

- enquire how the service charge is calculated;
- request to inspect accounts and receipts and make copies;
- challenge the landlord about the reasonableness of the level of the charge;
- demand prior consultation for major works.

If tenants consider that a particular cost was unjustifiably incurred or that it is unreasonably high, they can challenge it by action through the courts, having first attempted to solve the dispute by negotiation.

Tenants may request a summary of expenses on which the level of service charge is based, and any monies received but unspent. If there are more than four tenants in the block, the summary must be certified as fair by an accountant.

Variable service charge monies payable by more than one tenant must be held 'in trust' for the tenant. Holding the monies in trust means that the landlord or his agent has physical possession of the money, but it is for the benefit of the tenants until properly spent on the purposes of the trust, namely, care of the communal areas and the provision of communal facilities. This means that if the landlord or agent were declared bankrupt, the court would consider the money belonged to the tenants and would not distribute it among the landlord's creditors. It also prevents the landlord using the money for purposes other than service charge items.

Other arrangements

There are various other arrangements for the supply of communal services and the upkeep of communal areas, and you should discuss these with your solicitor. For example, if there are a number of flats it might be an idea to set up a company and transfer the communal areas to the company. The company's purpose is to tend the areas and organise the supply of services. Each tenant buys shares in the company and has a say in the running of it and how the matters are dealt with. Usually the landlord is on the board of directors of the company so he can still have a fair degree of control over the maintenance of the flats. The obvious disadvantage of this system is that running the company can be complex and time consuming. It is sometimes also difficult to get the tenants to take much interest in the running of the company. Also, as each tenant has a say, rather than the landlord being in full control, disputes may arise.

Insurance

It is vital that the block or conversion is properly insured. Usually this is the landlord's responsibility as he is in a position to be able to make certain that the entire building is comprehensively insured. The tenant can request a summary of information about the insurance, and in certain circumstances challenge it in court and request different arrangements be made.

Proper management of flats

Unless the landlord resides in the block, the tenants can apply to the court if there are two or more flats and they are being managed inadequately, to request that a manager is appointed. A court would consider whether the landlord has complied with his obligations under the lease and other relevant circumstances which would make the appointment of a manager necessary. In extreme cases, tenants who have long leases of over 21 years can apply to acquire the freehold interest inless the landlord is a resident landlord in a converted house.

Right to buy the freehold

Under the Leasehold Reform, Housing and Urban Development Act 1993, in certain circumstances the tenants have the right to form a group and ask the landlord to sell them the freehold, or an individual tenant may renew his lease. The tenants must have long leases of more than 21 years and the building must comprise at least two flats. The rent must be below a specified level. Usually a tenant of a long lease pays one large premium and then a low ground rent each year. As explained on pages 50–51, this book does not cover such leases in detail.

CHAPTER 8
Managing the property

Preparing the property for letting

Before you start to show prospective tenants around your house or flat you should ensure it looks attractive and that it is ready for the tenant to move in. Here is a check list of things that might need attention:

- rewiring of electricity;
- cleaning flues, checking radiators and boilers;
- redecorating;
- cleaning of carpets, curtains, linen and windows;
- ensuring locks work, getting extra keys cut for tenant;
- checking insurance arrangements;
- obtaining consent of your mortgagee if the property is mortgaged.

It is well worthwhile for the sake of your peace of mind and the tenant's safety to ask the local police to advise you about safety and security. Fitting extra locks and installing smoke alarms and a fire extinguisher are cheap things to do but could save lives and property.

Furnishing the property

If you are going to furnish the property you should choose the furnishings or alter the current furnishings to suit the kind of tenant you are hoping to attract. For example, a student will need a desk or writing table and bookshelves, but the furniture need only

69

be simple to keep the rent low. Below is a list of furnishings most tenants will expect. Items in brackets are optional. Remember, most tenants of short leases 'travel light' and may be put off the property if they have to buy many extras themselves.

Sitting room
sofa and armchairs
table
bookshelves
curtains
(pictures)
(lamps)

Kitchen
table and chairs
cupboards/shelves
cooker
fridge
freezer
washing machine
iron and ironing board
crockery
cutlery
cooking utensils
fire extinguisher
fire blanket
sink
waste bin
curtains/blinds

Bathroom
bath/shower
toilet
basin
bath mat

mirror
curtains/blinds

Miscellaneous
vacuum cleaner
dustpan and brush
mop and bucket
lightshades and bulbs
dustbin
instruction booklets for household equipment
at least two smoke detectors

Bedrooms
double/single bed
wardrobe
chest of drawers
curtains
(bed linen)
(writing table/desk)
(chair)
(bookshelves)
(lamp/study lamp)
(bedside cabinet)
(dressing table)

Hall
door bell/entry phone
telephone point
double lock on door
mirror
(cabinet/table)

Make sure that you prepare a detailed list or inventory of all the household items and the condition that they are in. For example, if a table is scratched, you might put 'slightly scratched' next to it. When the tenant moves in he must check the inventory and sign and return a copy of it to you. This will prevent arguments about the state of the furniture and the items provided at the end of the tenancy. As explained on pages 53–4, a tenant or licensee should pay for or repair any item that he wilfully damages or loses. If the item is replaced, it should be similar to and of the same standard as the original, and wording to this effect can be inserted in the lease or licence.

Consulting a solicitor and/or an estate agent

It may be a good idea to make this one of the first things that you do once you have decided to let your property. Your solicitor and estate agent will be able to advise you of the type of tenancy you should consider offering and your rights and obligations and those of the tenant. This advice should be tailor-made to your precise circumstances and the nature of your property.

Contact several solicitors and estate agents and compare quotes and prices. To ease the burden you should try to ask for a contribution towards the fees from the tenant. The tenant does not have to agree to pay a contribution, and usually for short lets it is no higher than about £60 to £70.

A solicitor will discuss the proposed tenancy with you and draft and explain the lease or licence to you. He will also deal with any assured shorthold notices or Ground 1 notices and send these and the draft agreement to the tenant or licensee directly or to his solicitor. When the agreement is returned, your solicitor will inform you of any amendments or deletions the other solicitor has made to the agreement, and he will negotiate the agreement and its terms until the draft is finalised.

Letting agents are usually part of estate agents. They charge either a flat fee or a percentage of the first month's rent. Again, you should compare prices and services. Using an agent to manage your property may be advisable if you are going to be a long way from the property, or if it is the first time you have let property and you would appreciate the support and advice of an agent.

Agents usually offer different levels of service. The basic service is to advertise the property, deal with enquiries, take up references of would-be occupiers, and arrange for the gas, electricity, water and telephone to be put in the occupier's name. They usually charge around 10 per cent for this. Drafting the legal document costs extra and is usually about £50 to £60 payable by both parties.

For a further 2 to 3 per cent, the agent will collect the rent. Full management of the property is about 15 to 20 per cent of the rent. For this the agent will offer all the above services and send an inventory clerk to the property to make a list of the contents. They will deal with the day-to-day management of the property – for example, the occupier will contact the agent not the landlord in the case of repairs. The agent will send their own contractor around to make the repairs having first agreed a fee, or it is sometimes possible for you to ask the agent always to use certain contractors specified by you.

Often agents will only be able to manage properties in a prescribed catchment area, and very often they will only take on property that is available for a minimum of six months or a year, and only if the owner agrees to create an assured shorthold tenancy.

Setting the rent or licence fee

The level of rent or licence fee you set should be high enough to at least cover your outgoings. You should therefore take into consideration:

- cost of any mortgage;
- insurance;
- tax;
- repairs;
- any management fee.

The rent or licence fee must be a good marketable rent or fee that will attract prospective occupiers. Rents and fees vary according to the location of the property, the type of property, its size and the quality and quantity of the furnishings. To get an idea of rents and fees, look at adverts in your local papers or call into an estate agents which deals with lettings.

There is no restriction on what licence fee you can charge for a licence, although obviously you have to come to an agreement which suits both you and the licensee. Licence fees are usually lower than rents because the licensee usually has just one room of his own, must share other facilities, and has no security of tenure.

There is no restriction on the initial rent you can charge for an assured tenancy, apart from market forces.

If the tenancy is an assured shorthold tenancy, the tenant can refer the rent to the Rent Assessment Committee as explained on page 40. However, the rent will only be reduced by the Committee if:

- there are a sufficient number of other assured tenancies or assured shorthold tenancies in the locality for a comparison to be made; and
- the rent is significantly higher than that which a landlord might reasonably expect to obtain.

An assured shorthold rent is less than the rent for a comparable assured tenancy because the assured shorthold tenant has limited security of tenure in comparison.

Collecting the rent or licence fee

Unless the agreement specifies that the rent or licence fee is payable in advance, it is payable in arrears. Most landlords and licensors insist on advance payment. The rent or licence fee should be a definite, not a variable amount, and should be payable at regular intervals such as weekly, four-weekly, per calendar month, quarterly (traditionally on 25 March, 24 June, 29 September, 25 December) six-monthly or annually.

Remember, if a statutory periodic tenancy arises because you allow the tenant to stay on after the fixed term ends, the period will be the interval at which rent is paid. The length of this period may affect the amount of notice that must be given to terminate the lease. The minimum amount of notice is usually four weeks, but under the common law you would have to give six months' notice for a yearly tenancy (for further details see page 84). Most landlords and licensors settle on monthly in advance, such as the first day of each month, and most tenants and licensees are happy to agree to this.

Rent or fees can be collected in a variety of ways:

- cash payment to you or your agent;
- cheque each month to you or your agent;
- standing order from tenant's or licensee's bank directly into your bank account.

The last method is by far the best because, unlike tenants or licensees, banks do not forget to pay the money! The sum will go straight into your account so you will not have any delay and consequential loss of interest. However, the occupier can, of course, cancel the standing order at any time. If you want to be paid by standing order you should insert words to this effect in the agreement, otherwise the tenant or licensee can insist on paying by any method he likes. If the rent is paid weekly, the landlord should provide a rent book, obtainable from most stationers.

Deposits

It is sensible to take a sum of money known as a deposit from a tenant or licensee. The agreement usually provides that the deposit will be returned at the end of the term, less any deductions made for non-payment of rent or licence fee, or damage to the property. When the deposit is returned it is not common practice to give interest on the deposit. However, there is no reason why the landlord could not put the sum in an interest-bearing account and give the tenant the interest. If the deposit is a considerable amount or will be held for quite a long time, the tenant or licensee may well ask the landlord or licensor to agree to this.

Sureties

Sureties or guarantors are not very common for short leases to individuals. The idea of having a surety is that if the tenant fails to pay the rent or carry out one of the covenants, the landlord can rely on the surety instead. The surety's obligations must be stated in the lease, and the surety must sign the lease. In practice, it may be difficult to find a tenant who will agree to provide a surety if he can easily rent a home from another landlord who does not request a surety.

Advertising the property

If you are using an agent, this will be done for you. Otherwise, consider these methods:

- local newspapers;
- national newspapers;
- card in newsagents;

- card in student union/your place of work;
- asking your friends and acquaintances whether they know of people who might be interested in the property.

The advert should have sufficient details to help people decide whether they are interested. Here are some examples you might like to follow:

Northwick: 2 bed spacious flat, second floor, kitchen, lounge, bath, share garden. Fully furnished, all mod cons. Nr. station. £600 pcm (per calendar month) exclusive of bills. Tel: 001-223 4545

Southminster: large fully furnished room in house for male aged 18-25. Share kitchen, bathroom, lounge with three students. 15 min walk to campus. £50 per week inclusive of bills. Tel: 879 3756

Westwood: Quiet, mature woman wanted to share house with female owner. Own room, share kitchen, bathroom, lounge. Near park. £60 per week incl bills. Tel: 683 4678

Easterly-upon-Sea: 5 bed house (2 double, 3 single). Suit family. 70 ft garden. Unfurnished. Minimum 5 year lease. Sea view, near shops. £800 pcm excl. Contact Mr. Worrier, Messrs Worrier & Fret 456 8364

Each advert above is designed to attract particular types of tenants. When people telephone to arrange an appointment, they will also usually ask further questions. Do not be afraid to ask preliminary questions yourself so that you can put off applicants you think would be unsuitable. You must be fair about this, obviously, and not prejudge people, but it would save time and bother if you asked questions, for example: 'Most people in the house are students aged around 18-22, and they are hoping to share with someone similar. Are you in that age group?' or 'The neighbours are rather elderly so I am hoping to let the property to a quiet couple with no pets. Could I ask whether that description would suit you?'

Showing the property

Besides being a chance for the applicants to decide about the property, it is also a chance for you to decide whether they would be suitable tenants for the property. As you will probably be showing around a lot of people, make a conscious effort to remember who each person is. Keep a careful record of their names and where they can be contacted.

Things to remember when showing the property include:

- show each room and draw attention to facilities (such as dishwasher, Economy 7 electricity);
- mention the neighbours;
- give details about local transport, shops, entertainment;
- say how much the council tax is;
- say what is the minimum and maximum length of lease or licence you are prepared to offer;
- mention whether pets are allowed;
- explain rent and deposit details.

Things to ask prospective tenants or licensees:

- how long they want the property for;
- employment/study/other occupation;
- whether they can provide references;
- general conversation to get to know a bit about them.

As mentioned in Chapter 2, you must be sure that neither you nor your agent creates an informal or oral agreement by accident when showing the applicants around. Terms should be discussed in principle only, nothing should be agreed at this stage, and no money accepted.

Choosing a tenant

The following advice applies equally to choosing a licensee but you should also refer to the special considerations detailed in Chapter 3.

Be fussy! If you do not think you have found the right tenant, re-advertise if necessary. Once you have decided to offer the property to someone, contact him to see if he is still interested. Make sure that he understands that the offer is subject to agreeing the lease and taking up satisfactory references.

Send the tenant a copy of the lease and ask him, or them if more than one, to provide names, addresses and telephone numbers of referees. You should obtain references from:

- current or recent landlord;

- current employer/principal of college;
- bank or building society.

Once the references have proved satisfactory and the lease has been agreed in principle, you will need to give him notice of an assured shorthold tenancy, or Ground 1 notice if appropriate (or other notices, see pages 86–92). Make sure the lease is correctly dated and signed by all parties and that you have retained a signed copy for yourself.

When the tenant moves in

Arrange to meet the tenant on the day the tenancy commences. The following matters should be dealt with:

- signing of the lease;
- receive a cheque for: deposit
   one month's rent in advance
   contribution to legal fees;
- hand over the keys;
- give the tenant standing order details and forms if appropriate;
- check and sign inventory and copy;
- explain how household equipment works;
- explain security measures;
- explain fire escape route;
- explain what to do and who to contact in the event of ordinary repairs and emergency repairs.

It is sensible to put up a list of useful information and telephone numbers of people such as the landlord, agent and emergency repair contractor. In the event of ordinary repairs, the tenant should notify the landlord or the agent. However, in the event of an emergency the tenant will need to contact someone immediately and perhaps out of office hours. The landlord could agree with the tenant that, in an emergency, he can contact a certain repair firm. The firm or individual should be specified by the landlord so he can ensure that they are reputable and charge a reasonable price. Either agree with the firm in advance that invoices should be sent directly to the landlord, or, if that is not possible because payment is required on the spot, agree that the tenant will pay for the repairs but the landlord will reimburse him on presentation of the invoice which should show all details of the repair and why it was necessary.

Alternatively you could allow the tenant to deduct the repair costs from the rent, but this would not give you the opportunity of refusing to pay for the repairs because they were unnecessary or were the tenant's own fault and should be paid for by him. You would have to ask for the reduced rent to be paid in full, and this could lead to long arguments with you out of pocket in the meantime.

'DSS' tenants

Some landlords advertise their properties with a statement 'DSS tenants not accepted'. By this they mean that they do not want a tenant who is unemployed and living on income support or unemployment benefit paid by the Department of Social Security. Such people may be entitled to claim housing benefit from the local council to pay the rent. They can choose either to receive the money themselves, or ask the council to pay the money to the landlord directly. If the landlord receives the rent directly from the council or if the tenant can be relied upon to use the money to pay the rent, there is no reason why the landlord cannot be sure that the rent will be paid.

Some landlords prefer not to accept tenants who are unemployed because they are worried that the tenant will fall behind with the rent. If the rent is not paid, there is no hope of claiming it through the courts as there is no point suing someone who has no income or savings. Some landlords might not like the idea of the tenant being in the property all day long, and others may be prejudiced against unemployed people. However, unemployment can happen to anyone at any time. An employed tenant could lose his job and claim housing benefit and you might not even know this has happened as the council will not inform you. As long as the rent is being paid, you cannot ask the tenant to leave the property.

By contrast, some landlords positively welcome DSS tenants and provide much needed good accommodation, knowing that if they persuade the tenant to ask the council to pay the rent directly to the landlord, the rent will continue to be paid regularly and promptly until the tenant finds work and pays the rent himself.

If the council considers that the rent is too high for the type of accommodation, or that the accommodation is too large for the tenant's needs, it will only pay the amount of rent it considers reasonable. This is to avoid unscrupulous landlords setting up a scheme to obtain unrealistically high rents which they could not charge in the private sector.

If you are happy to let your property to a person who is unemployed, you might consider enquiring whether your local council would take on the letting for you. If they agree, the council will usually find the tenants, deal with all the practical and legal aspects, and promise to return the property to you in its original condition (if necessary the council will repair the property if the tenants cannot).

Maintaining the property

As explained on page 54, a lease usually obliges a tenant to notify the landlord of any repairs that need to be done. It is important that repairs and general maintenance are carried out promptly so as not to allow the property to run into a state of disrepair. You should therefore include a clause in the lease similar to the one set out below:

> The tenant will permit the landlord or the landlord's agent on reasonable notice and at reasonable hours to enter the property to view its state and condition.

As a lease gives the tenant exclusive possession it is necessary to insert a clause to this effect to give the landlord and his agents access from time to time. It is a good idea to make this viewing a regular event. You will then be able to ensure that the property is being cared for in a tenant-like manner, and the tenant will have the opportunity of raising any matters about the house or flat that he would like to discuss.

Increasing the rent

If the lease is for more than one year you will want to have the option of increasing the rent to allow for inflation and changes in the rented property market.

If the lease is for a fixed term the law says that rent cannot be altered during the term unless the lease provides for that increase or the tenant voluntarily agrees to pay more rent. As it is rather unlikely that the tenant will agree voluntarily to an increase, it is sensible to provide for one in the lease along the following lines:

> The rent shall be increased on the * day of * 199*, and on the * day of * in each succeeding year, by a sum to be determined by the landlord.

or:

> The rent shall be increased on the * day of * 199*, and on the * day of * in each succeeding year, by the same proportion as the retail prices index for the month preceding the increase bears to the retail prices index for the same month in the previous year.

Assured tenancies
During the original fixed term
As explained in Chapter 4 the rent agreed for a fixed term assured tenancy cannot be assessed and changed by the Rent Assessment Committee, and this is so even if there is a rent review clause. To raise the rent during the fixed term, therefore, all you need to do is firstly ensure that there is a rent review clause, and then notify the tenant of the increase in accordance with the clause (usually at least one month's notice of the increase is given).

If the tenancy is not a fixed term tenancy but is instead periodic, the rent can be increased as if the tenancy were a statutory periodic tenancy discussed below.

After the fixed term expires and a statutory periodic tenancy arises
If the tenancy is not brought to an end after the expiry of the original fixed term, a statutory periodic tenancy will arise as explained in Chapter 3. The landlord can increase the rent but, if the tenant chooses to, he can ask the Rent Assessment Committee to review it.

You cannot charge the new rent until either the first anniversary of the date on which the tenancy originally began, or the first anniversary of the last previous increase, whichever is the later. Following a determination by the Rent Assessment Committee, you cannot increase the rent again for a further 12 months.

MANAGING THE PROPERTY

Example:
Laura's lease began on 1 April 1989 and expired on 31 March 1993. She has stayed in the property under a statutory periodic tenancy. On 1 April 1993 the landlord can raise the rent. Laura can refer this to the Rent Assessment Committee.

The landlord can next raise the rent on 1 April 1994, and again Laura can refer the increase to the Rent Assessment Committee.

However, the landlord does not raise the rent until 2 May 1994. The landlord can only next raise the rent on 2 May 1995.

Notice of the increase
The landlord must give the tenant advance notice of the increase in rent. The notice period depends on the type of periodic tenancy. As explained on page 20, the tenancy will be periodic according to the interval at which rent is paid. The following amounts of notice should be given:

Type of periodic tenancy	Amount of notice
Yearly	six months
Six-monthly	six months
Quarterly	one quarter
Monthly or weekly	one month

The increased rent will take effect from the date stated in the notice unless the landlord and tenant agree otherwise, or the tenant requests that the Rent Assessment Committee should state a later date.

The Rent Assessment Committee will disregard any effect on the rentable value of the property which may be due to:

- the fact that the property has a sitting tenant;
- any improvements to the property which the tenant has made;
- any failure of the tenant to comply with the terms of the lease (for example, the tenant has neglected the property).

There are special preprinted forms of notice of increase in rent which you should complete and serve upon the tenant. The notice will remind the tenant of his right to refer the increase to the Rent Assessment Committee. If the tenant agrees to the increase he need not do anything. If he disagrees, he should try to come to some agreement with the landlord and, failing that, refer the notice of the increase to the Rent Assessment Committee before the date on which the new rent is payable.

Assured shorthold tenancies
During the original fixed term
The tenant can ask the Rent Assessment Committee to review the rent originally agreed. If the Committee does determine what the rent should be, the rent cannot be increased at all during the original fixed term, whatever the lease may say.

This inability to raise the rent during the original fixed term following a determination by the Rent Assessment Committee is a good reason for not making 'long' assured shorthold tenancies. It is a good idea if the first fixed term is for no longer than 12 months. If the assured shorthold tenancy is for longer than 12 months, you should include a break clause in the lease enabling you to end the lease before the term expires. Then, if the tenant should obtain a determination by the Rent Assessment Committee, you have the option of ending the lease and granting a new lease (to the same tenant if you so wish).

It is not possible to create a periodic assured shorthold tenancy if it is the first term to be offered to the tenant.

After the fixed term expires
When the fixed term expires you can either allow the tenant to stay on under a statutory periodic tenancy, or you can immediately grant a new fixed term assured shorthold tenancy.

Statutory periodic tenancy
If you allow the tenant to stay on with a statutory periodic tenancy, the rules for increasing the rent are the same as for statutory periodic tenancies arising after an assured tenancy ends (see page 80). However, if the tenant seeks a determination of the rent during the statutory periodic tenancy, it is simpler to end the tenancy if the original lease was an assured shorthold tenancy. As explained on page 92, when an assured shorthold tenancy expires you have an absolute right to possession of the property and do not need to prove a special ground to the court.

Subsequent fixed term
If you grant another fixed term assured shorthold tenancy to the tenant after the expiry of the original term, you can set the rent and increase it in accordance with the new lease as you wish. The

tenant cannot ask the Rent Assessment Committee to review the rent of any assured shorthold tenancy which is subsequent to an original fixed term. The new term must be created immediately the old one expires, otherwise a statutory periodic tenancy will arise.

In practice, many landlords opt for one of the following arrangements:

1. Grant a six-month to one-year assured shorthold tenancy and when it expires, allow the tenant to stay on with a statutory periodic tenancy and raise the rent. If the tenant goes to the Rent Assessment Committee, the landlord can end the tenancy if necessary. He can then re-let the property. The landlord should bear in mind that if the Rent Assessment Committee has decided the rent was too high, re-letting at the same high rent may cause the new tenant to request the Rent Assessment Committee to review the rent.

2. Grant a six-month to one-year assured shorthold tenancy and when it expires, offer the tenant a new six-month to one-year assured shorthold tenancy.

3. Grant a two- to five-year assured shorthold tenancy with rent review provisions and a break clause.

Students and other young people 'on the move' are usually happy to accept options 1 and 2. Tenants who want a more secure home will usually prefer option 3 or request an assured tenancy as these offer more certainty that the tenant can stay in the property for a good length of time.

Licences

As the Housing Act 1988 does not affect licences for rent review purposes, the licensor can simply raise the licence fee in accordance with the terms of the agreement, or by separate agreement with the licensee. At least one month's notice of the proposed increase should be given to the licensee. As it is relatively simple to end a licence, the tenant may want to leave if the licence fee is put up unreasonably high, so the licensor should bear this in mind and set a fair level of licence fee.

CHAPTER 9
Termination and renewal

This chapter considers the 'life cycle' of a tenancy or licence. The agreement may simply run its course and both parties will need to decide whether to terminate or renew it. Both parties might want to terminate the agreement before it comes to an end, or one party may want to terminate the agreement unilaterally. What options are available will depend on the type of tenancy (if it is a tenancy and not a licence) and the rights of the parties under the agreement and according to the law.

Termination by the tenant

Periodic tenancies
The tenancy may be periodic either because the landlord expressly created a periodic tenancy or because the fixed term has expired and a periodic tenancy is implied by statute. The tenant can end the tenancy either by giving notice according to common law, or by giving notice in accordance with the terms of the lease.

Under common law the length of the notice must be:

Type of periodic tenancy	Notice period
Yearly	six months' notice expiring at the end of the lease's year
Six-monthly	six months
Quarterly	quarterly
Monthly or less	one month

Alternatively, the tenant can terminate the lease according to any special terms in the lease. For example, the lease might permit a shorter notice period.

If there is no special term in the lease, the landlord and tenant could come to a separate agreement as to how the lease may be terminated by the tenant if this is not to be carried out according to the common law. This is known as an agreement to surrender the lease. Unscrupulous landlords might make a tenant enter into such an agreement before the commencement date of the tenancy, so that the tenant is obliged to surrender the lease at a later date in accordance with the prior agreement. This would deprive the tenant of his statutory rights of security of tenure, therefore any agreement of this kind which is entered into before the tenancy commences is void by law.

Fixed term tenancies
The tenant can make an agreement to surrender the lease as explained above. Alternatively the lease may provide a break clause. Remember that, for assured shorthold tenancies, the break clause must not be operable before a minimum of six months from the start of the lease. The notice should specifically refer to the break clause in the lease for the sake of certainty.

Effect of the tenant terminating the lease
Once a tenant has terminated the lease he loses all rights of security of tenure under the Housing Act. He must vacate the property at the agreed date at the end of the notice period.

The tenant cannot terminate the lease by any other method than those described above. The tenant is contractually obliged to see out the end of the term. If he tries to give notice wrongly and vacates the property, the landlord can still demand rent until the end of the term.

Assured tenancies - termination by the landlord
If the landlord wants to terminate the tenancy, he must apply to the court for an order. The order will only be granted if one of the special grounds in the Housing Act can be proved. Obtaining a court order is the only way to end the tenant's right to occupy the

property under the Act, if it is the landlord who wants to end the tenancy.

Periodic tenancies including statutory periodic tenancies
A notice to quit given by the landlord will have no effect. To end the tenancy a court order must be obtained and until then the tenant will have a right to occupy the property.

Fixed term tenancies
A fixed term may terminate because the term has come to an end or because the landlord has given notice according to a break clause in the lease. Although the original lease will then cease to exist, the tenant will still have a right to occupy the property. If the landlord does not offer a new lease immediately after the end of the expired lease, a statutory periodic lease will be implied under the Housing Act. The statutory periodic lease will start immediately after the end of the expired lease. The terms of the periodic lease will be the same as the old lease, but any term permitting termination in the old lease cannot be applied to the new periodic lease. The only way to terminate a statutory periodic lease is to obtain a court order.

The grounds for possession

Before applying to the court the landlord must fill in a special preprinted form of notice (obtainable from stationers or from your solicitor) and serve it on the tenant. The notice must contain the following particulars:

- that the landlord is seeking possession of the property;
- the ground on which possession is sought, and details of the ground;
- the earliest date on which the landlord may start proceedings for the court order. The very earliest date is two weeks from the date of service of the notice on the tenant, but some grounds (1, 2, 5, 6, 7 and 16) require at least two months' notice. Additionally, if the tenancy is periodic, the notice must be at least the length of notice required under the common law (see page 84);
- the latest date for commencement of proceedings (usually 12 months after service of the notice).

TERMINATION AND RENEWAL

In some cases the court may agree that a shorter notice period is given if the situation is particularly urgent, unless the landlord is using Ground 8.

The grounds are divided into mandatory grounds and discretionary grounds. If a mandatory ground is proved by the landlord, the court must grant a possession order. If a discretionary ground is proved, the court will only grant an order if it considers it is fair and equitable or reasonable in all the circumstances to do so.

Which ground to use

If the tenancy is an express periodic tenancy or is a statutory periodic tenancy, any ground can be used. If the tenancy is a fixed term tenancy and still existing, only Grounds 2, 8 and 10 to 15 can be used. More than one ground can be used.

The landlord must be absolutely sure that he has reasons to support the ground or grounds he is relying on. If the landlord obtains possession by misrepresenting or concealing the facts, the tenant can apply for substantial compensation.

If the tenant has lawfully sub-let the property to an assured sub-tenant, when the original tenant's tenancy terminates the sub-tenant will become an assured tenant of the landlord as the original tenant drops out of the picture. If, however, it is impossible due to one of the statutory exceptions (such as the landlord living in the property) for the sub-tenant to be an assured tenant, the sub-tenant will not have the protection of the Act. For example:

> Lawrence lets part of his own house, which he resides in, to Tom. Tom moves out and sub-lets to Sally on an assured tenancy. Lawrence terminates Tom's lease, leaving Sally as his direct tenant and no longer Tom's sub-tenant. Sally's lease cannot be an assured tenancy because her landlord now lives in the property. Lawrence can then terminate Sally's lease without having to prove a ground.

Mandatory grounds

1. Owner occupier

This ground can only be used if notice that possession might be sought under this ground was given before the start of the tenancy (see Chapter 4). In some circumstances the court will waive the need to have given notice but only if it is considered just to do so.

A possession order will be granted if either:

(a) The landlord occupied the property as his only or main residence at some time before the start of the tenancy. If there is more than one landlord only one needs to have occupied the property for the ground to apply.

The landlord does not have to have occupied the property immediately before the tenancy was granted; it is sufficient if he has lived there genuinely as his main residence at any time before the tenancy was created. The landlord does not need to show why he wants the property back. It could be, for example, that he wants to sell it rather than live in it again.

or

(b) The landlord (or one of the landlords, or the landlord's spouse) requires the property as his only or main home.

This case will need to be used if the landlord did not previously occupy the property as his main home. However, the ground cannot be used if the landlord bought the property when it was subject to the tenancy, or acquired it somehow from a landlord who bought the property when it was subject to the tenancy. This rule is to prevent people from buying tenanted property only to evict the tenant and live there themselves. If the property was acquired other than by purchase, for example, the property was inherited, the ground can be used as long as the new landlord genuinely wants to live in the property as his residence.

2. Mortgagee's power of sale

The landlord's mortgagee (for example, his bank or building society) can require possession of the property in order to exercise its power of sale. For example, the mortgagee will have a right to exercise the power if the landlord does not make his mortgage repayments. The mortgagee must prove that a Ground 1 notice had been given when the property was mortgaged, or ask the court to dispense with the need for such a notice.

3. Out of season accommodation

The landlord is entitled to possession if:

- the tenancy is for a fixed term but no longer than eight months; *and*
- the property was occupied under a holiday letting; *and*
- prior to the start of the lease the landlord gave the tenant notice that possession might be required under this ground.

4. Out of term time student accommodation

This can only be used by landlords who are an educational establishment as specified by the Act; it does not apply to ordinary landlords letting property to students. The establishment can obtain possession if the fixed term lease is no longer than 12 months and, within 12 months prior to the tenancy, the property had been let to a student. Usually this ground is used when student accommodation is let to other tenants during vacations.

5. Minister of religion's house

If the minister of religion gave notice prior to the tenancy commencing, he can recover possession of the property if it is required for his duties.

6. Reconstruction, substantial works, demolition

The landlord can gain possession if:

- he can show to the court that he honestly intends to demolish, reconstruct, or carry out substantial works to all or part of the property. The landlord should provide some evidence for this intention, for example, planning permission; *and*
- the work cannot reasonably be carried out unless the landlord has vacant possession.

A landlord cannot use this ground if he bought the tenanted property or acquired it somehow from a landlord who bought the property while it was tenanted.

A landlord granted a possession order under Ground 6 must pay the tenant's reasonable removal costs.

7. Death of periodic tenant

When the tenant dies the property will be in the hands of his personal representatives or administrators who will deal with the deceased's estate according to the will or to the laws of intestacy if there is no will. The Act permits only the spouse, or the person who lived with the deceased as a spouse, to succeed to the property. If the landlord brings proceedings within 12 months of the death, he will be granted possession. The landlord cannot use this ground if he grants a new tenancy to the successor, or varies the old tenancy agreement. In these specific circumstances, merely accepting rent from the spouse will not create a new tenancy.

8. Substantial rent arrears
What is substantial depends on how the rent is paid:

Rent interval	Substantial arrears
weekly or fortnightly	13 weeks
monthly	three months
quarterly	one quarter's rent is three months in arrears
yearly	three months' rent is in arrears for three months.

The landlord will gain possession if:

- the rent is lawfully due. Money lawfully deducted from the rent by the tenant (for example, to carry out repairs which should have been done by the landlord) will not count as rent for these purposes; *and*

- the rent is in arrears at the date when the landlord serves notice and at the date when proceedings commence. This rule can be vexing as the tenant can pay up at the last minute. However, the landlord might be able to use the discretionary Grounds 10 and 11 below; *and*

- where the tenancy is fixed term, the lease provides that Ground 8 may be used during the term, or the lease provides that the landlord may forfeit the lease and re-enter the property in the case of rent arrears.

Discretionary grounds

9. Suitable alternative accommodation
If the landlord can show that he can offer the tenant alternative accommodation that is similar to the current accommodation and suitable the landlord can ask the court to consider granting possession of the property currently occupied by the tenant.

10. Rent arrears
If rent is lawfully due but unpaid at the date of service of the notice of intention to take proceedings, the landlord may seek possession. Even if the tenant pays the arrears by the time the court proceedings commence, the court may still consider granting the landlord possession, unlike the mandatory Ground 8. Ground 10 can be used during the term of a fixed term tenancy as long as the lease provides for termination or forfeiture in the event of rent arrears.

11. Persistent delay in paying rent
If the tenant delays paying rent on at least more than one occasion, this is a ground for seeking possession.

12. Breach of obligations
This ground may be useful where the tenant has not complied with the obligations in the lease. For example, the tenant might not be carrying out repairs, or he may be keeping pets contrary to the terms of the lease. Whether the court grants possession will depend on the nature of the obligation, how seriously it has been breached, and whether the tenant could make amends.

13. Waste or neglect
If, due to the tenant's neglect or default, the property deteriorates, the landlord can seek possession. If the tenant's lodger or sub-tenant causes the waste or neglect to occur and the tenant does not remove the lodger or sub-tenant, the landlord can seek possession under this ground.

14. Nuisance
This ground covers cases where the tenant is being a nuisance to people living in adjoining accommodation. It also applies where the tenant is convicted of illegal or immoral use of the house, such as prostitution or drug trafficking.

15. Damage to landlord's furniture
This is the same as Ground 13 but applies specifically to the furniture and effects provided by the landlord for the tenant's use. The deterioration or damage must result from ill treatment by the tenant or his lodger, sub-tenant or guest, not from normal wear and tear.

16. Tenant is former employee of the landlord
This ground may only be used where the property was originally let to the tenant because he was employed by the landlord (or the landlord's predecessor). If employment ceases, possession may be sought. The ground can only be used for fixed term tenancies still running if the lease has a break clause entitling the landlord to terminate the lease.

Assured shorthold tenancies - termination by the landlord

Possession may be recovered from assured shorthold tenancies on any of the 16 grounds applicable to assured tenancies. If the landlord wants to regain possession during the fixed term of the tenancy, his only means of gaining it is by using one of the applicable grounds.

If the landlord wants to regain possession after the end of the fixed term, or during a periodic tenancy, one of the grounds may be used, or the landlord can follow a special procedure available only to assured shorthold tenancies. This procedure is as follows:

Fixed-term tenancies
When a fixed term tenancy comes to an end, the landlord has the following options available to him:

- grant a new fixed term;
- grant a new periodic tenancy (periodic assured shorthold tenancies can only be created after the expiry of the initial fixed term tenancy);
- allow the tenant to stay on under a statutory periodic tenancy; or
- terminate the tenancy.

Terminating the tenancy is very simple. All the landlord needs to do is to serve a notice on the tenant at least two months before the fixed term is due to expire, stating that possession is required in not less than two months' time, that is, possession is required on the date of the expiry of the term. Usually tenants leave the property of their own accord at the end of the term having received such notice. However, if they do not leave, they will be entitled to continue to occupy the property until a court order for

TERMINATION AND RENEWAL

possession is obtained. As long as the landlord can prove service of the notice to terminate the fixed term tenancy, the court must grant an order for possession. The landlord does not need to prove any special ground to obtain possession. Service of the notice can be proved by showing the court a copy of the notice signed by the tenant to acknowledge safe receipt of the notice.

Periodic tenancies including statutory periodic tenancies

Again the landlord must serve a notice to end the tenancy. The notice must state that possession is required on a specified date. This date must be a date:

- which is at least two months after the date of service of the notice; *and*

- which is the last day of a period of the tenancy (for example, if the period is monthly, the date must be the end of the month); *and*

- which is not earlier than the date on which a landlord could obtain possession under the common law (see page 84 for these notice periods). This means that, if the period is quarterly, the termination date must be at the end of the next quarter. A whole quarter's notice must be given instead of the minimum two months' notice. Many leases specifically exclude the need to give common law notice so that only the minimum notice need be given whatever the length of the period.

As with fixed term tenancies, once a court order for possession is obtained, the tenant has no right to occupy and must leave.

Examples

Mark has a monthly periodic tenancy with rent being payable on the first of each month. It is now the end of February 1993 and Gwen wants to terminate Mark's tenancy. She must give notice to Mark not later than 31 March 1993 in order to terminate the tenancy in two months' time on 31 May 1993.

Teresa has a quarterly periodic tenancy with rent being payable on the usual quarter days. It is now 1 April 1993 and Martin wants to terminate Teresa's tenancy. He must give notice not later than 24 June 1993 (the next quarter day) in order to terminate the tenancy on 29 September 1993 (the following quarter day).

Practical aspects of terminating a tenancy

Once it has been decided to end the tenant's occupation of the property, some practical matters must be considered:

- ensuring the property is left in a good condition;
- returning any deposit paid by the tenant and any excess rent;
- re-letting the property.

Re-letting

Once the termination date has been decided it is a good idea to make two appointments with the tenant to view the property and its contents. The first appointment should be as soon as possible and the second appointment should be the date the tenant vacates the property.

The first appointment should be to check the general condition so that any repairs can be made and to check the property is in a good state for prospective tenants to be shown around. If anything is seriously amiss with the property as a result of the tenant breaching any of his covenants, an early viewing appointment will give you time to take action before the tenant moves away (see Chapter 10 on problem tenants).

The lease should specifically entitle the landlord to show prospective tenants around either personally or accompanied by an agent. You should decide when the property will next be available for occupation. If many repairs and decorations need to be done it might not be available immediately after the tenant vacates. You might also decide to renovate the property and provide new furniture and facilities so that a higher rent can be charged. If this is the case you will probably prefer to show prospective tenants around once the work has been completed. If you do show tenants around while the current tenant is in occupation, you should agree with him at what hours the property may be viewed. Additionally, you should give the tenant some advance warning that the property needs to be available for showing so that the tenant is not unduly disrupted and also so that, it is to be hoped, he will tidy up the property.

If you have developed a good relationship with the tenant and consider him trustworthy, it may be worth enquiring whether he is aware of any acquaintances who would be interested in renting the property.

Financial matters
The following matters will need attention:
- arrange for telephone, gas and electricity meters to be read and a bill sent to the tenant;
- if water rates have been paid by the tenant, agree that a rebate will be paid in proportion to the length of non-occupation; if water rates have not been paid but are due, arrange that the tenant pays for the amount of time he has occupied the property;
- if rent has been over- or underpaid, arrange for a rebate or payment as appropriate;
- at the first viewing appointment ask the tenant to make repairs or replacements of damaged or lost items due to the tenant's wilful neglect, and to clean and tidy the property;
- at the second viewing appointment on vacation of the property, check whether repairs, replacements and cleaning have been carried out satisfactorily and that rent is paid up to date. If everything is satisfactory, the deposit can be returned in full. If only rent is outstanding, deduct outstanding rent from the deposit. If repairs, replacements and cleaning have not been seen to, the deposit should not be returned until these have been completed and the cost known.

Vacation of the property
If the tenant vacates the property earlier than the agreed date, he is still liable for the rent. The tenant should inform you of the date and time of his expected departure and a mutually convenient appointment to view the property should be made, preferably just before the tenant vacates the property. At this meeting the following should be seen to:
- outstanding financial matters;
- thorough check of furniture and household effects and their condition against the inventory. Once checked, the landlord and tenant should again sign and date the original inventory and

copy, and a note of any agreement as to payment for repairs or replacements or cleaning should be made;
- ensure that furniture is in the correct position;
- ensure that the tenant removes or properly disposes of all personal belongings and rubbish;
- make a note of tenant's new address (to forward mail, unpaid bills etc.);
- turn off water mains if property will be left unoccupied for some while;
- tenant should return keys and copies he has made. If he does not, you should change the locks and deduct the cost from the deposit.

Renewing a tenancy

If the tenancy is coming to an end and both you and the tenant are happy that the tenancy should continue, there are several options:

- grant a new fixed term tenancy;
- grant a new periodic tenancy;
- allow a statutory periodic tenancy to arise.

New fixed term tenancy

The procedure for granting a new fixed term tenancy will be the same as for terminating a tenancy and granting a new tenancy. You will need to bring the old tenancy to an end, though this should be achieved by agreement and you will not need to obtain a court order for possession. The inventory should be checked and any necessary action taken just as if the tenant were leaving, though the deposit need not be returned.

A new lease will need to be drawn up and completed. This can be almost identical to the old one if wished, but you may wish to alter some of the terms or insert new terms to reflect any change in circumstances. You may also wish to increase the rent (see Chapter 8).

If the old tenancy was an assured tenancy, a notice of an assured shorthold tenancy must be given before the old tenancy expires if you agree that the type of tenancy should change.

If the old tenancy was an assured shorthold tenancy and you want to change it to an assured tenancy, you must give notice that the new tenancy is to be assured.

The advantages of creating a new fixed term are:

- certainty of terms and conditions;
- certainty as to length of the new term;
- no rent restrictions on an assured shorthold fixed term tenancy that follows an original assured shorthold tenancy;
- no rent restrictions on a fixed term assured tenancy.

The disadvantages of creating a new fixed term are:

- expense of creating a new lease (but it should not be very expensive as the parties are the same);
- length of term is relatively inflexible compared to periodic tenancies;
- when one fixed term expires and both parties still want the tenancy to continue another tenancy must be created or a statutory periodic tenancy allowed to arise.

Express periodic tenancy
Although an original assured shorthold tenancy cannot be periodic, both an assured tenancy and an assured shorthold tenancy following an original fixed term can be periodic. As when creating a new fixed term, the old lease will have to be terminated, and the inventory checked.

The advantages of creating an express periodic tenancy are:

- certainty as to what the terms are as there will be a written lease;
- new terms can be agreed and a new rent set;
- periodic tenancies are flexible and they can continue indefinitely.

The disadvantages of creating an express periodic tenancy are:

- slight expense of creating a new lease;

- rent restrictions (see Chapter 8).

Statutory periodic tenancy
As explained earlier, a statutory periodic tenancy will arise automatically if the tenant stays on after the fixed term lease expires. The terms will be the same as those in the old lease, and the period will be according to the interval at which rent is paid.

The advantages of a statutory periodic tenancy are:

- there is no need (and therefore no expense) to do anything to create a statutory periodic tenancy;
- the length of term is flexible as with express periodic leases.

The disadvantages of a statutory periodic tenancy are:

- terms in the old lease which are inconsistent with a periodic lease will not apply – this may lead to uncertainty;
- rent restrictions (see Chapter 8).

New terms can only be introduced and existing terms varied in accordance with statutory rules. The landlord or tenant must serve a special preprinted notice on the other party stating what the proposed new terms or the variations are. If the recipient does nothing, after three months the proposed terms will become part of the terms of the tenancy. If there is a dispute which cannot be negotiated between the parties, the recipient can refer the proposed terms to the Rent Assessment Committee within three months of receipt of the notice. The Committee will consider whether the terms or variations to the terms are those that might reasonably be expected to be found in an assured periodic tenancy of that sort of property.

Terminating a tenancy or licence which is not under the Housing Act

The commonest situation where the tenancy is outside the Housing Act is where a home owner lives in his home and lets a room to a tenant or lodger (see page 32). These tenancies can be terminated by giving a notice to quit, but the tenant or licensee cannot be made to leave or be evicted without a court order (see pages 111–12).

The notice to quit must contain information prescribed by law.

Specially preprinted forms can be obtained from most large stationers. The information should include:

- a statement that the landlord requires the tenant or licensor to deliver up the property and a statement of the details of the property;
- the date on which the property must be delivered up or vacated;
- the date of the notice to quit;
- a statement that the landlord or licensor must apply for an order for possession if the tenant or licensee does not leave the property, and that the landlord or licensor cannot apply for the order until the notice to quit has expired (that is, the date on which the tenant or licensee should vacate the property has passed);
- a statement that the tenant or licensee should seek legal advice.

The notice to quit should be given in accordance with the common law, or in accordance with any prior agreement. The common law requirements for periodic leases or licences are as set out on page 84. If the tenancy is a fixed term, at least four weeks' notice before the date of expiry of the term should be given. By law, no less than four weeks' notice should be given, even if, for example, the tenancy or licence is weekly.

The notice to quit should be signed and dated by the landlord and served upon the tenant or licensee. Ideally you should serve it on the recipient personally and ask him to sign and date it together with a copy for you to keep as acknowledgement of receipt. If the notice to quit is served incorrectly or is wrong in any way, the court will not grant an order for possession should the tenant or licensee not go of his own accord and you need to evict him.

If the tenant does not leave the property after the expiry of the notice and/or after the expiry of the fixed term lease or licence and you continue to collect rent or licence fees, an implied periodic tenancy or licence could arise (see pages 20–21). If an implied lease or licence arises, you will need to serve another notice to quit. It is therefore safer not to accept rent once the notice has expired. Instead you will be entitled to compensation for the use of the property beyond the date on which the tenant or licensee should have left – this compensation is known as 'mesne profits' and is awarded by the court.

What if the tenant or licensee wants to quit?

As with tenancies under the Housing Act, the tenant or licensee is contractually obliged to see out the term if it is fixed unless the parties agree otherwise. If the lease or licence is periodic, the tenant can leave only after giving due notice in accordance with the common law or with the terms of the agreement.

Renewal of the tenancy or licence

If a fixed term tenancy or licence is due to expire but both parties wish for the occupation to continue, it is best to draw up a fresh agreement. If a fresh agreement it not created but rent or licence fees are still accepted, an implied periodic lease or licence will arise as explained above. The terms will be the same as the expired agreement. However, new terms can 'creep in' to the agreement as there is no special procedure for varying terms or introducing new ones as with tenancies under the Housing Act. For example, the tenant or licensee may start using the garden whereas this was not permitted under the old agreement. If you agree to this either expressly or by implication, use of the garden could arguably become a term of the new lease or licence.

CHAPTER 10
Problem tenants and licensees

If, despite having chosen your tenant or licensee carefully, problems arise, you will want to put an end to them as quickly as possible. You will need to decide whether the problem can be managed by yourself and the tenancy or licence allowed to continue, or whether the agreement should be ended. This chapter looks at self-help remedies and taking legal action.

The commonest problems are rent or licence fee payments, damage or neglect of property and creating a nuisance.

Rent or licence fee problems

The tenant or licensee may be either failing to pay the entire rent or licence fee, or part of it, or persistently delaying payment. The causes are numerous and may include forgetfulness, hardship, disagreement about the level of rent or licence fee, or simply wishing to inconvenience the landlord or licensor.

As we saw in Chapter 8, the best way to prevent this problem is by following these guidelines:

- select the tenant or lodger carefully;
- state a definite rent or licence fee and payment dates in the agreement;
- provide for a clear method of increasing the rent or licence fee in the agreement (or by using the special procedures for assured tenancies and assured shorthold tenancies);

- impose a penalty interest rate for late payment;
- state a method of payment, preferably standing order;
- state in the agreement that in the event of non-payment, the landlord may re-enter the property and determine or forfeit the lease or the licensor may terminate the licence.

These steps will also help you to solve payment problems amicably or by going to court.

For both leases and licences, it may be possible to argue that there is an implied term that the tenancy or licence will be terminated if the rent or licence fee is not paid.

Self-help solutions

Discuss the problem with the occupier. If the cause of delay is simply forgetfulness, arrange for a standing order to be made. Emphasise that the rent or licence fee must be paid on time otherwise interest may be payable or the agreement terminated.

If this does not work you will need to be firmer. Give the tenant or licensee a statement showing when rent or licence fees were due, when they were paid and when they were not paid, and the interest now payable on the arrears. Inform the tenant or licensee that unless the arrears and interest are paid you will have to consider legal action.

The problem may be genuine hardship or poor control of personal finances. If the former, advise the occupier that he could be eligible for housing benefit and should consult the local council's housing benefit office. If the latter, suggest a standing order is implemented. An agreement should be made as to how the arrears and interest can be paid – either in one lump sum or by regular instalments, preferably by standing order.

Suing in court for an unpaid debt

The first thing you must bear in mind is that there is absolutely no point suing if the debtor has no money. Try to ascertain whether he is employed and/or receives other income, whether he has any valuable assets, such as a car, or property elsewhere. If he is unlikely to have any financial resources, it is best to accept your losses and obtain possession of the property.

If, however, you do decide it is worth going to court, you should also consider the solicitor's fees and court costs as these are not fully recoverable even if you do win; in some cases they may not be recoverable at all. If you are fortunate, the threat of legal action or the arrival of a writ or summons may be enough to make the debtor pay. He must also pay for the cost of the writ or summons.

Before taking legal action, first determine exactly how much is outstanding and how long it has been outstanding. Check the provisions of the lease or licence for payment methods and dates and interest. Obtain as much information as you can, and seek proper legal advice from a solicitor. Your local Citizens' Advice Bureau will be able to advise you initially as to your rights. Inform the debtor of your intention to take legal action. In addition to this your solicitor will send the debtor a 'seven day warning letter' which will inform him that, unless the arrears and interest are paid by a certain date, legal action will be commenced. The letter should state exactly how much is outstanding, how interest is calculated, details of the lease or licence and of the property. If a service charge is payable, as long as the lease states that it is payable as rent, the overdue service charge can be claimed with the rent and possession may be obtained on the grounds of non-payment of the charge.

Depending on how much is outstanding and the complexity of the situation, if the debtor does not pay up and the case goes to court, it will be heard in the 'Small Claims Court', County Court or High Court.

The Small Claims Court
This court, which is part of the County Court, is for claims up to £1000. Claims above that amount can be heard in the Small Claims Court if the parties agree. The advantage of bringing a claim in this court is that it is much cheaper and much less formal than the other courts.

Cases are heard by the District Judge who acts as an arbitrator rather than a traditional judge. It is not necessary to have a lawyer to speak for you. Instead it is usual for each side to present their own case. If there is someone who can give evidence for you, you can call them as a witness.

The cost of bringing an action rises according to the amount you want to claim. Costs range from £7.00 to £43.00 (1993) which is obviously much cheaper than costs in the County Court and High Court. Unlike the higher courts, if you lose your case you will not have to pay the other side's costs. Do not forget, though, if you do employ a solicitor, you will have to pay his fees, and you will not be able to recoup them or obtain a contribution towards them from the losing party in the Small Claims Court.

The County Court staff will give you the necessary forms to complete in order to bring a claim, and they will also explain the procedure to you if you wish to represent yourself.

The County Court
The County Court hears most landlord and tenant disputes, for example, possession actions and debt claims. The County Court hears more complex cases and more expensive claims than the Small Claims Court.

Cases are heard by either a judge or a registrar (a 'junior judge'). After judgement there may be an award for one party to pay the other's costs. An appeal can be made to the Court of Appeal if there is a dispute about a point of law, evidence or procedure.

The High Court
This court is for claims worth more than £50,000 and very complex cases. The High Court is divided into three divisions. Cases involving the law of contract, tort and the recovery of land are held in the Queen's Bench Division (the other divisions are Chancery, which deals with financial matters such as mortgages, wills and bankruptcy, and the Family Division).

Methods of enforcing payment
Garnishee proceedings
This is commonly known as freezing a bank account, but other sums of money can be frozen: for example, if the debtor is owed money by a business, the business can be ordered to freeze that sum instead of paying it to the debtor. The debtor will not be able to cash cheques or withdraw money on a frozen bank account. The bank or business is known as the garnishee.

Once the sum has been frozen, a hearing at court is held which both the creditor and debtor attend. Unless there is a good reason to the contrary, the court will order that the frozen sum is paid directly to the creditor.

This method is very useful if it is known that the debtor has money in an account or is owed money. As it is not necessary to obtain the debtor's consent to the freezing of the sum, the debtor has little chance of disposing of the money elsewhere to avoid the order.

Seizing goods
This is known as a 'writ of fieri facias' in the High Court and a 'warrant of execution' in the County Court, but it is basically the same process.

When the writ or warrant has been obtained, a Sheriff's officer (High Court) or Court bailiff (County Court) will go to the debtor's property. The officer or bailiff is entitled to seize any valuable goods except bedding, clothing or a person's tools of trade, for auction to pay the debt. Usually the goods are not taken away instantly but instead an inventory and valuation is made. This gives the debtor some time to pay the debt rather than have his goods auctioned. Many debtors do pay up as an auction will not raise the full value of the items which may also have sentimental value to the owner. Once the inventory is made, the debtor cannot remove the goods. The next stage is that the goods are taken away by the officer or bailiff, but again a few days are allowed for the debtor to pay up before the auction is held.

This method is only practical if you know that the debtor has goods of sufficient value. Problems and delays can occur if the debtor removes the goods or alleges to the officer or bailiff that they do not belong to him.

Charging order
This method is often not useful in landlord and tenant cases as it requires the debtor to have land and usually the reason the tenant is renting property is because he does not own any himself. The order can also be placed over stocks and shares. The order, which is only available in the High Court, is not a means of securing immediate payment of the debt. If a charging order is made, a charge is registered on the land or securities so that, when they are sold or transferred in the future, the creditor must be paid out of the proceeds of sale.

Attachment of earnings
This is a method of obtaining payment directly out of a person's wages before they are paid to him by his employer. The order can only be obtained in the County Court.

The debtor will be required to complete a questionnaire about his earnings and expenses (such as a mortgage, living expenses and number of dependants). Sometimes a questionnaire is also sent to the debtor's employer for verification of the employee's wages. Often the threat of applying for the order will be sufficient to make the debtor pay to avoid the embarrassment of the employer discovering that his employee is not honouring his debts.

If the court registrar has enough information he will make a provisional order deducting a certain amount from the debtor's wages each month until the debt is paid. If the registrar does not have sufficient details he can order a hearing to obtain more information. If the creditor or debtor wishes to challenge the order he can request a hearing.

This method is obviously only possible if the debtor has a job. It cannot be used against a self-employed debtor. Even if the debtor does have a job he may lose it. His personal circumstances may change and he may ask the court to reduce the amount paid each month in view of his increased personal liabilities. The debtor might also change jobs or move address and be difficult to trace.

Possession action – assured tenancies and assured shorthold tenancies

If you require possession of the property and an end to the tenancy, you should make an application under one of the grounds in the Housing Act (see pages 87–92). The applicable grounds are Ground 8 (substantial rent arrears), Ground 10 (rent arrears), and/or Ground 11 (persistent delay in paying rent). If the tenancy is a periodic or statutory periodic assured shorthold tenancy and you have decided to cut your losses and forgo the arrears, notice to terminate the tenancy may be given and a possession order obtained without having to prove a ground (if the lease is a fixed term and is still running you will need to prove a ground). If the tenant has refused to pay rent, you should seriously consider ending the tenancy to avoid further non-payments of rent.

Possession action – tenancies outside the Housing Act and licences

If you wish to end the occupation you must give notice as specified in the agreement or according to the common law. See page 84 for details of giving these notices. Note that, if the tenant or licensee does not leave of his own accord, you will need to obtain a possession order from the court in order to evict him (see pages 111–12).

Breach of covenant

A covenant is a contract and if the tenant or licensee breaches a covenant, he is liable for damages. Depending on the terms of the agreement, it may also be possible to terminate the tenancy or licence.

Whether you decide to take legal action will depend on how important the covenant is, and how serious the breach is. Some covenants may be difficult to enforce by law as it might not be easy to know when or whether they have been performed (such as covenants to clean the windows every four weeks, not to keep pets, not to keep food in the bedroom). Breach of such covenants may not be considered very serious by the court and damages would be nominal either because breach of the covenant would not adversely affect the property or the landlord's interest or because the degree of the breach is minor such as the tenant's petty repairs being left undone for a while.

The covenant may, however, be very important and the breach severe. Repairing covenants, covenants concerning illegal use or use of fire and flammable materials would come under this category. In these circumstances you should probably be prepared to take legal action if self-help remedies do not prove successful.

Self-help solution
Make an appointment to see the tenant or licensee and the property or room. It is important to establish exactly what covenants have been breached and how badly. You should make a note of the meeting. The lease should state that the landlord is entitled to enter the property to view its condition. A licensee has no exclusive possession and should permit the licensor to enter at a convenient time.

Remind the occupier of his obligations, referring to the agreement if necessary. Tell the occupier exactly what needs to be done, or, depending on the nature of the problem, what the occupier should refrain from doing. Agree a date when the breach should be put right. The occupier might not have been aware of his obligations or how to carry them out correctly.

After the visit, write to the occupier and summarise what happened at the meeting and what was agreed. Keep a copy of this letter. Attach a list of all repairs that need to be carried out. Arrange in advance another appointment to check that the covenant has been properly observed. For a tenant who is obliged to carry out repairs, a written repair notice should be given and a reasonable date specified for completion.

Legal action and possession proceedings
An action for damages or for 'specific performance' (making the tenant do something that he is obliged to do) or an injunction (preventing the tenant from doing something he should not do) can be sought through the courts. This will take time and there is no guarantee that another or a different problem will not occur. Usually, if the situation cannot be resolved amicably, the landlord or licensor will want to obtain possession.

Assured tenancies and assured shorthold tenancies
If possession is required, Ground 12 (breach of obligations) and/or Ground 13 (waste or neglect) should be used (see page 91). If the tenancy is a periodic tenancy or a statutory periodic assured shorthold tenancy and you simply want the tenant to leave, notice to terminate the tenancy can be served and a mandatory possession order obtained (see Chapter 9).

Tenancies outside the Housing Act
The lease must provide that, if the covenant is breached, the property may be re-entered and the lease determined. If this is not possible, you may be able simply to give notice to terminate if the tenancy is periodic, or if the lease provides a break clause you could use that.

Licences
If the licence is periodic you can simply give notice to terminate the licence according to the length of the licence period. If the licence is fixed, strictly speaking you are contractually obliged to permit the licensor to reside for that length of time, unless the licence has a break clause or it permits termination for breach of a term. You could also attempt to come to an agreement to terminate the licence.

Causing a nuisance

This is likely to be a breach of an express term of the agreement, or it could be argued that there is an implied term that the occupier should not cause a nuisance. Accordingly the same action as for breach of covenant above may be taken, except that the ground for nuisance applies to assured tenancies and assured shorthold tenancies (Ground 14).

If the tenant or licensee is causing a nuisance, such as playing loud music at unsocial hours or creating other disturbances, it is worth having a frank discussion with him and advising him of the consequences of not taking heed of the warning. However, the problem may be of a more permanent nature and the best solution may be to terminate the agreement before other tenants or licensees hand in their notice and neighbours start complaining.

Some local councils have a tenancy relations officer who can intervene in these situations. Environmental Health Officers at the local council can also take action against the offender if he is making an unreasonable noise.

Physical violence to the person or property should be dealt with firmly and promptly and the police informed. It may be possible to get a swift eviction order in these circumstances.

Harassment and eviction

The law against illegal eviction and harassment (the Protection from Eviction Act 1977 and the Housing Act 1988) applies to all residential tenancies and licences. These are criminal offences which can carry a penalty of a fine and imprisonment.

A case may be brought by the occupier or by the local authority. The local authority can investigate suspected instances of harassment and eviction and prosecute the landlord or licensor, and they also have the power to impose a control order and manage poorly run multiple occupation lets. The occupier may be entitled to monetary compensation and the right to live in the property again.

Harassment

A landlord (or his agent, that is, someone who acts on his behalf by his authority) commits the offence if he:

(a) does acts likely to interfere with the peace or comfort of the occupier or members of his household; or

(b) persistently withdraws or withholds services reasonably needed by the tenant to live in the property as a residence,

and the landlord knows (or has reasonable cause to believe) that such behaviour is likely to cause the occupier to:

- leave the property; or
- give up part of the property; or
- stop doing things he has a right to do or pursuing remedies in respect of the property.

The landlord or licensor may be able to defend his actions if he can prove that he had reasonable grounds for doing (a) or (b) above. For example, he might have cut off the water supply because he thought the occupier had left.

Examples of things that might amount to harassment
Physical or verbal abuse
The behaviour might relate directly to wanting the occupier to leave, or it may be indirect and designed to make the occupier feel frightened or insecure. An occupier who is threatened or caused a nuisance by someone on behalf of the landlord or licensor can also take action for harassment. For example, the neighbours might be incited to behave in a way that makes the occupier want to leave.

Withholding or withdrawing services
The landlord or licensor must not cut off supplies to the house or flat such as water, gas or electricity. This includes allowing the various companies responsible for the supplies to cut them off because the landlord or licensor has failed to pay the bill (when the landlord or licensor is responsible for paying the bill). The occupier can ask the local authority to restore the services and charge the landlord or licensor.

Problems concerning repairs
A landlord or licensor must not allow the property to get into a state of disrepair that would cause the occupier discomfort and be likely to make him or her want to leave. Nor should he start

repairs or renovations and leave them undone to inconvenience the occupier, or try to make the occupier carry out unreasonably expensive or unnecessary repairs. There may, however, be a genuine reason for the repairs or renovations being left undone or incomplete – lack of planning permission, or illness of the landlord or licensor, for example. This would not amount to harassment, but the landlord or licensor or his agent should rectify the situation as soon as possible.

These instances could also amount to:

- breach of covenant by the landlord;
- a wrong or 'tort' under the law or nuisance or negligence;
- sexual or racial harassment; or
- assault.

Eviction

A landlord or licensor must give the occupier proper notice to leave the premises. In the case of tenancies under the Housing Act, a notice of intention to take legal proceedings must be given. For other tenancies and licences, notice to quit of not less than four weeks must be given according to the common law or to the agreement (see page 84).

A court order must be obtained in most cases to evict the occupier. Even if the term has expired and the notice to quit has expired, the occupier has a right to remain until an eviction order is obtained and the occupier must not be harassed into leaving before then. Having said that, most occupiers do move on of their own volition.

A court order does not have to be obtained in the following cases:

- if the landlord or licensor is resident in the property as his only or main home;
- holiday accommodation;
- if the occupier is in fact a trespasser;
- other cases such as various lettings by councils and housing charities.

If, having obtained the order, the occupier still does not leave, a court bailiff will force the occupier to vacate the premises. It is unwise to attempt to make the occupier leave yourself instead of using a court bailiff, as the occupier may have an action against you if you cause him personal injury or damage his property.

Summary

Having warned in this chapter of the problems that might occur, it should be emphasised that most well organised residential arrangements run smoothly. As long as proper legal advice is obtained before the property is let, the occupier is chosen carefully, the owner follows the correct procedures during the course of the occupation and carries out his obligations diligently and promptly, letting property can be a very rewarding business. As well as solicitors, your letting agent, Citizens' Advice Bureaux and your local council and court can provide advice and information.

Glossary

The following is a glossary of some of the terms and phrases used in landlord and tenant law.

Act of God Unforeseen disastrous events caused by nature. Insurance policies may not cover such events.

Agent A landlord may appoint an agent to act on his behalf. The landlord is known as the principal and he is bound by the acts carried out by the agent.

Agreement An agreement is made when two or more people consent about something. The agreement might not amount to a contract (see below), and may instead be a purely voluntary agreement which, in most cases, cannot be enforced by law.

Arrears A tenant or licensee who is in arrears has not paid money which is legally charged and due.

Assignment When a tenant assigns his lease to another, the assignee, he transfers his legal rights to the assignee. The assignee takes the place of the tenant and becomes the direct tenant of the landlord.

Assured shorthold tenancy This is a species of assured tenancy. Despite its name, the tenancy can be for any length of time, but it must be at least six months long. The initial term offered to the tenant must be fixed and not periodic. To end the tenancy, the landlord need only prove that it has been properly terminated, or he can also prove a special ground where applicable.

Assured tenancy   A tenancy under the Housing Act 1988. Tenancies usually come under the Act if the property is a separate dwelling house let to an individual person for the purposes of his main residential home. The tenancy may be for a fixed term or periodic. It may only be ended if the landlord follows a special procedure and proves a Ground specified by the Act for termination.

Attachment of earnings   This is a method of obtaining payment of a debt by obtaining a court order that directs that a certain amount is deducted from the debtor's wages each month. It does not apply to self-employed people.

Bailiff   A court bailiff is a person employed by the County Court to enforce court orders and carry out various duties. For example, a bailiff is able to seize the tenant's goods for payment, and evict a tenant. In the High Court these duties are carried out by the Sheriff's Officer.

Beneficial owner   See *Trust*

Bona fide   Latin for 'good faith'. A common use of this term is for a bona fide purchaser without notice, which means that the person bought the goods or property honestly and in good faith without being aware of any fault with them.

Breach   This term is used when a person has broken his obligations. The obligation may be a contract, covenant or term. Once a breach has occurred, the injured party is able to enforce his rights or seek compensation, and in some contract cases he can terminate the contract.

Charging order   This is a method of securing payment of a debt by attaching an order to land or securities so that, when they are sold or transferred, the creditor is paid out of the proceeds.

Chattel   A chattel is any property other than land. A chattel real is an interest in property (as opposed to the freehold). A chattel personal is a movable object such as a water butt, or furniture, or an intangible object which has value such as the goodwill of a business.

GLOSSARY

Closing order The courts may make a closing order to prevent people from occupying a building if it is considered that there is a grave risk of fire or if it is unfit for human habitation.

Common law Common law is the law that has evolved throughout the centuries by judges trying cases. Principles of law develop from the cases. The circumstances of the cases and the decisions set precedents which are followed in similar cases. Some areas of the law are governed by both statutory law and the common law.

Communal areas These are areas of a house or flat or its grounds which are used in common by all or some of the occupants.

Community charge This charge replaced rates and was set by the local authority. It was commonly known as the poll tax. It was a personal charge borne by individuals. In April 1993 it was replaced by the council tax.

Compensation Compensation is money awarded by a court to compensate or attempt to put right a wrong. In contract law the compensation will be calculated to put the wronged party in the position he would have been in had the contract been performed properly. In tort, the compensation aims to put the person in the position he would have been in if the wrong had not happened. Compensation may be reduced if the court considers that the wronged person could have mitigated his circumstances or made them less bad by taking simple steps.

Contract A contract is an agreement which legally binds the parties. It consists of an offer which is accepted in return for providing consideration. Consideration is something which has monetary value such as money itself, or an object, or doing something valuable such as mowing the lawn in return for the loan of some deck chairs. The contract may be oral ('by word of mouth') or express (written) or both. Some contracts, such as a lease for more than three years, must be in writing.

Council tax The tax introduced in April 1993 to replace the community charge. It is a personal tax rather than a

115

property tax, but it is based on the value of the house or flat. The tenant or licensee is liable to pay this tax in most situations.

Covenant A covenant is a term in a contract or deed which obliges someone to do something (a positive covenant) or refrain from doing something (a restrictive covenant). Breach of covenant may, in some circumstances, entitle the wronged party to terminate the contract.

Damages Damages are similar to compensation and may be ordered by the court to be paid to the wronged party in tort or contract cases. If the loss or injury is minor, the damages may only be nominal or very small.

Default A tenant or licensee defaults when he fails to honour a legal obligation such as an obligation to pay rent or make repairs.

Demise Demised property means let property.

Deposit A deposit is a sum of money, usually one month's rent or licence fee, which is held by the landlord on trust. At the end of the tenancy or licence, the landlord or licensee may deduct sums from the deposit if rent is unpaid or the occupier has breached his obligations. If no sums are to be deducted, or if money remains after the deduction has been made, the deposit must be returned to the tenant or licensee, though it need not be returned with interest unless the agreement provides for this.

Determine A person determines a tenancy or licence when he terminates it or brings it to an end.

Devise A person devises property when he passes it on to another by will. The recipient is known as the devisee. Property other than land is left by a legacy and the recipient known as a legatee.

Distress Distress is levied on property when goods are seized as payment for a debt or obligation which has not been fulfilled.

Draft A draft agreement is the rough lease or licence which passes between the parties until the terms have been agreed. The draft is unsigned and undated and is not legally enforceable.

Easement   An easement is a right which is attached to a particular piece of land rather than a right given to the public at large. For example, the tenant may have an easement which grants him the right to use another's path, whereas the public may have a general right of way over a particular track of land such as a public footpath.

Encumbrance   An encumbrance is a right over a piece of land when the right is not for the benefit of the owner. For example, land is encumbered when it is mortgaged to a bank.

Enfranchisement   Certain tenants are entitled to enfranchise or free their leases by purchasing the freehold from the landlord.

Estate   This word can be used to describe the land itself, but it can also be used to refer to the type of interest, such as freehold or leasehold that a person has in the land.

Eviction   A person is illegally evicted if his landlord or licensor or their agents makes the occupier leave when he has a right to stay there. It is a criminal offence. A person can only be legally evicted if the landlord or licensor gives proper notice to terminate the agreement and an eviction order is obtained from the court.

Exclusive possession   If a person has the right to exclude others from his property he has the right to exclusive possession. This is one of the main tests as to whether the person has a lease or licence. A licensee does not have exclusive possession, and the licensor can admit others to the premises.

Execution   An agreement is said to be executed when it is properly signed and dated. The document is then legally valid.

Express   An express agreement is one that is overtly made by the parties as opposed to being implied by the law to exist due to the circumstances.

Fieri facias A writ of fieri facias is the High Court method of seizing goods to pay for a debt.

Fitness for habitation A local authority may take action if rented property is not fit for human habitation. The property should be damp-free, well lit and ventilated and have good sanitation, drainage, water supplies and cooking facilities.

Fitness for purpose It is an implied term of a licence that the property is fit for the purpose of the licence.

Fixed term A fixed term has a definite beginning and ending stated in the agreement. The initial term offered to an assured shorthold tenant must be fixed.

Fixtures and fittings Fixtures and fittings, unlike chattels, are fixed and not movable. Wallpaper and piping are fixtures, for example.

Forfeiture A landlord is entitled to forfeit a lease or 'take it away' in some circumstances, for example, if the lease provides that the lease may be forfeited in the event of non-payment of rent.

Freehold The freeholder is the person who owns the property 'outright' and is not beholden to any landlord.

Frustration An agreement is said to be frustrated or broken if an unforeseen event which neither party has any control over occurs and makes it impossible or illegal to perform the contract, or if the contract were performed it would be very different from what was originally intended. If a contract is frustrated, both parties are freed from their obligations. If one party has received money from the other, that should be returned. An example of frustration would be someone agreeing to hire a hall for a dance but before the dance the hall is struck by lightning and is burnt to the ground.

Garnishee proceedings This is a method of forcing a debtor to pay what is due by freezing a bank account or other sum of money so that the debtor has no access to it. The sum or a portion of it is then ordered to be paid to the creditor instead.

Ground 1 notice   This is a notice given by a landlord to warn the tenant before the tenancy begins that possession might be sought under this ground in the Housing Act 1988. The ground relates to requiring the property as it is the landlord's and/or his spouse's main residential home.

Harassment   Harassment is a criminal offence and is committed by a landlord/licensor if he or his agent interferes with the peace and comfort of the occupier or withdraws essential services to the property with a view to making the tenant want to leave the property.

Holding over   An occupier holds over when his agreement has expired but he continues to live in the property. Usually an implied lease or licence or a statutory periodic tenancy arises.

Holiday accommodation   Accommodation which is let for a fixed term of no more than eight months for the purpose of a holiday counts as holiday accommodation under Ground 3 of the Housing Act and if the landlord gives advance notice that possession may be required under this ground, the court must grant the landlord a possession order.

Housing benefit   People who are unemployed or receiving income support or are on a low income may be entitled to housing benefit payments from their local authority. The payments are for rent or the licence fee and are paid either to the occupier or the landlord or licensor.

Implied lease/licence/term/covenant   In certain circumstances the law will say that something exists even though there is no express or written proof to show that it does exist. For example, if a tenant pays rent every month to his landlord, the law will imply a monthly periodic tenancy. If a lease or licence is silent as to whether an important term such as quiet enjoyment or assignment exists, that term will be implied into the agreement.

Injunction   An injunction is a court order which prevents someone from doing something which he is not meant to do.

Joint and several liability   If people are jointly liable, they are responsible for each other's actions and defaults and all or any of them can be pursued by the landlord or licensee. If there is only several liability, each person is liable only for his own acts or defaults. If there is both joint and several liability, each is responsible for his own actions and defaults as well as everyone else's.

Keeping a disorderly house   It is a criminal offence to run a brothel.

Law of equity   Equity is composed of various principles which have developed over the centuries like the common law. Equity is based on what is the right and just thing to do in all the circumstances of the case.

Lease   A lease is an interest in land for a certain length of time granted by the freeholder or the superior leaseholder (someone who has a longer lease than the lease being granted) otherwise known as the landlord or lessor, to the tenant or lessee in return for rent. A tenant has the right to exclusive possession.

Licence   A licence is an agreement between the licensor and the licensee which permits the licensee to live in the property and distinguishes him from a trespasser. The licensee pays the licensor a licence fee (otherwise it is known as a bare licence). A licensee has no right to exclusive possession, and no security of tenure although he is protected from illegal eviction and harassment.

Lodger   A lodger is a licensee who receives services such as bed-making, laundry and meals from his landlord.

Mesne profits   If an occupier stays on in property when he is not entitled to do so, the owner is entitled to monetary compensation known as mesne profits for the use of the property.

Multiple occupation   A house or flat is said to be multiply occupied if individuals live in the property separately from each other. They will have separate agreements with the licensor or landlord, and they will have several liability only.

Notice   There are many different kinds of notice which must be given to a tenant or licensee, for example, notice that the tenancy is to be an assured shorthold tenancy, Ground 1 notice, Ground 8 notice, notice to carry out repairs, notice that the landlord intends to take legal proceedings for possession, and notice to quit. There are special rules governing each kind of notice, when and how it is to be given and what sort of information should be contained in it. If the notice is given wrongly or is incorrect in some way, in some circumstances, such as a notice to quit, the court will consider it invalid and the notice must be served again.

Nuisance   Nuisance (Ground 14 under the Housing Act) may entitle the landlord to possession. There is also nuisance under the law of tort, and local authorities have special powers in the case of nuisance due to loud noise.

Occupier's liability   By statute, an occupier is liable if damage, injury or death is caused to people who enter the property, or damage to personal property. The latter may be excluded in a contract, but not the former.

Operative part   The operative part of a lease is the part which sets out the rights and obligations of the parties.

Oral agreement   An oral agreement is by word of mouth, although it may be evidenced in writing, that is, a note of what was agreed orally may be made. The note does not constitute a contract.

Overcrowding   A house under multiple occupation must not be overcrowded. The basic test is that two or more people of the opposite sex who are not married or living together as if married, should not have to share a room. There should also be enough toilets and bathrooms for the number of people in the house.

Periodic tenancy or licence   A periodic tenancy or licence is one that runs from period to period until brought to an end by either party. Unlike a fixed term, it does not have a specified end. The period is usually according to how often the rent is paid, so if the rent is paid monthly, the period will be monthly. A periodic tenancy may be express or implied. The first term of an assured shorthold tenancy cannot be periodic, but subsequent agreements can be.

Planning permission   Many changes, developments, alterations or extensions to property need planning permission from the local authority, and it is an offence to build or change a property without first having obtained the permission. Permission is also necessary if the use of the property is being changed, for example, an office is being changed into a dwelling house.

Possession order   A landlord who requires his property back and an end to the tenancy must apply for a possession order. Without such an order, the tenant is entitled to remain in the property.

Protected tenancy   This is a tenancy which is protected by the Rent Act 1977. The landlord can only obtain possession if he proves certain specified grounds and the tenant is able to apply for a fair rent to be registered which may be below the market rent for letting such a property. These sorts of tenancy are still in existence, but it has not been possible to create one since 15 January 1989.

Quarter days   The traditional days on which rent is paid under a quarterly tenancy are 25 March, 24 June, 29 September and 25 December. Different quarter days can be stipulated in the agreement.

Quiet enjoyment   This is the right which is implied into all leases that the tenant should be able to enjoy or live in the property without interference from people claiming other rights over the property.

Quit   Notice to quit can be given by either a tenant, a licensee, a landlord or a licensor. The notice must be in accordance with the common law or with the agreement, and if the landlord or licensor gives the notice, it should be no less than four weeks long.

Recitals   The descriptive part of a lease which names the parties and the property let.

Re-enter   Many landlords provide a right to re-enter the property and forfeit or terminate the lease. This gives the landlord the right to take up possession of the property, as long as the proper statutory procedure is followed.

GLOSSARY

Rent Assessment Committee   The Committee is composed of experts and lay people and sits to determine a market rent if so requested by a tenant. It also considers new terms or changes to existing terms which the landlord or tenant wish to introduce.

Reversion   The reversion of a property is the interest retained by someone who lets it to another. For example, if a freeholder creates a lease, that lease will come to an end, and the freeholder will have the property back. While the lease still exists, the freeholder is said to own the reversionary interest in the property. The reversionary interest may be sold to another person.

Seizing goods   A method of obtaining payment for a debt by taking the goods of the debtor for auction.

Service charge   A charge imposed on tenants who live in a flat or a conversion of a house into flats to cover the expenses of maintaining communal areas and supplying communal services.

Set off   This is where a debtor owes money for something, but claims that the debtor's creditor also owes him money for something else. The debtor will argue that he should be able to deduct what the creditor owes him from his own debt to reduce it or nullify it, or result in the creditor having to make an additional payment if the sum is not sufficient.

Sheriff's officer   See *Bailiff*.

Small Claims Court   This court deals with claims worth £1000 or less and is part of the County Court. It is a relatively cheap and quick means of settling a dispute and is less formal than other courts.

Specific performance   This is a court order which forces someone to do what he is obliged to do under an agreement.

Stamp duty   Some documents require a tax known as stamp duty to be paid in order for them to be a valid evidence of title. The tax is either in proportion to the value of the transaction, or is at a fixed rate of 50 pence.

Statutory law   Statutory law is the law made by Acts of Parliament. The statutes or Acts may be updated or altered by statutory instruments which supplement each Act and are passed from time to time.

Statutory periodic tenancy When an assured tenant or an assured shorthold tenant remains in the property after the expiry of the term of the lease, a periodic tenancy will be implied by statute (the Housing Act 1988). The terms are the same as those under the old lease. The tenant is entitled to stay in the property until the landlord obtains a possession order, or the tenant gives due notice to quit.

Sub-let A tenant who lets the whole or part of his property to another tenant becomes a landlord himself. The new tenant is known as the sub-tenant or sub-lessee. As there are now two landlords, the original or first landlord is known as the superior landlord, being a landlord who has a superior interest in the land, and the new landlord is the inferior landlord. The inferior landlord remains a tenant of the superior landlord. In some cases, if the original tenant (the inferior landlord) leaves or has his lease forfeited, the sub-tenant will become the immediate tenant of the superior landlord.

Tenant-like manner A tenant should look after the property in this manner, which means caring for it, cleaning it and doing odd small repairs as he would look after his own home.

Tenants' association This is an association set up by tenants who all have the same landlord to deal with common interests such as the maintenance of communal areas and supplies.

Tort A tort is basically a wrong. Negligence, nuisance, personal injury and defamation come under this branch of law. The wronged person is entitled to damages to compensate him for his loss or injury.

Trespasser A trespasser is someone who has no legal right to be on the property. Trespass is a tort, and in some cases it is also a crime.

Trust If a person holds property, including money, on trust for another (the beneficiary) he must deal with that property for the benefit of the person and in a manner befitting the purpose of the trust. The trustee must act responsibly and follow the rules set down by law. The trust may be express, that is, created by individuals, or it may be implied by law according to the circumstances of the case.

Use classes All property is designated a use class for the purposes of planning permission which specifies what the property may be used as. If the owner wishes to change from one use class to another, such as from a shop to a residence, he must obtain permission from the local authority.

Vacant possession A property is said to have vacant possession if there is no one occupying it. There may, however, be other people who have rights over the property even though they do not live there.

Waste or neglect A tenant must not commit waste or permit another person to, nor must he neglect the property. He must not, for example, chop down trees, dispose of furniture or allow the property to fall into a state of disrepair because he has failed to care for it in a tenant-like manner. Waste or neglect is a ground for possession under the Housing Act.

Wear and tear An agreement usually requires the occupier to return the property to the landlord or licensor in the same condition as it was at the commencement of the tenancy or licence, but fair or reasonable wear and tear is usually excepted. Faded curtains or chairs broken due to old age rather than wilful neglect or misuse will not therefore need to be replaced or mended by the occupier.

Yield up This means that the occupier should give up the property to the landlord or licensor at the end of the term, but it does not free the landlord or licensor of his responsibilities under the Housing Act or the Protection from Eviction Act.

Index

advertising 74–5
agreement to surrender 85
alterations to property 55
assignment 55
assured and assured shorthold tenancies:
   assured tenancies and assured shortholds compared 40
   break clauses 42
   buying freehold 68
   creating assured shorthold tenancies 43
   creating assured tenancies 43, 50
   examples 41–2
   increasing rent *see* rent
   letting own property 44–5
   minimum term of assured shorthold tenancy 40
   notice of an assured shorthold 43, 71, 77
   periodic assured shortholds 92
   rent 40, 72–3
   repair 53
attachment of earnings order 105–6

bills 35, 59–60
   household items 36
   included in rent 59–60
   kitty 36
break clause 42, 85

charging order 105
communal areas *see* service charge
communal rooms 28, 48–9
council tax 59
County Court 104

covenant 107
   breach of 107
   effectiveness 60–61
   enforcement 52, 107, 108

debt action 102–6
deposits:
   collecting 74
   returning 94, 95

easements 63
enfranchisements 51, 68
estate agent 12–13, 62, 71–2
eviction 111–12
exclusive possession 30, 50, 79, 107

fire prevention *see* security and safety
fitness for habitation 57–8
freehold 17–19
   flying freehold 19
   right to buy 68
furnishings:
   damage to *see* repair and maintenance
   effect on rent or licence fee 15
   for room or house 27–8, 69–70
   inventories 70–71, 95
   tax implications 15
   wear and tear 55

garnishee proceedings 104–5
Ground 1 notice 44, 71
grounds for possession:
   assured tenancies and assured shorthold tenancies compared 39
   breach of obligations 108
   damage to landlord's furniture 91

INDEX

death of periodic tenant 89
discretionary grounds 90–92
effect on sub-lease 87
false grounds 87
Ground 1 notice 44, 71
letting your own home 44, 71
mandatory grounds 87–90
minister of religion's house 89
mortgagee's power of sale 88
nuisance 91
out of season accommodation 88
out of term time student accommodation 89
owner occupier 87
particulars of notice 86
persistent delay in paying rent 106
possession action 39, 106–7
reconstruction, substantial works, demolition 89
rent arrears 91, 106
statutory periodic tenancies 39
substantial rent arrears 90, 106
suitable alternative accommodation 90
tenant is former employee of landlord 92
waste or neglect 108
guests 33–4, 52, 56

harassment:
  definition 110
  examples 110–11
  penalties 109
High Court 104
holiday accommodation 20, 38, 111
household rules:
  examples 60–61
  multiple lets 49
  own house 32–6
Housing Act 1988:
  application 38
  avoidance 24, 38
  licences 32
  purpose 11, 23
housing benefit 78–9, 102

income tax 13, 15–16
insurance 29
  blocks of flats 67
  validity of policy 29

joint and several liability 48

Landlord and Tenant Act (1954) 51
Landlord and Tenant Act (1985) 53, 64
Landlord and Tenant Act (1987) 68

leaseholds 18–19
  letting leasehold property 19
letting agent *see* estate agent
licence:
  fitness, safety and suitability of property 57–8
  fixed term 31
  lease or licence? 30–32, 49–50
  letting own home 30–32
  lodgings 30
  multiple lets 49–50
  no exclusive possession 30, 107
  periodic licence 31
  termination 31, 98–9
  terms of agreement 31
licence fee:
  accepting fee after term ends 100
  default 101
  increasing fee 32, 83
  interest on fee 102
  no security of tenure 30, 73
  payment 73
  setting level 32, 72
  varying terms 100
lodgings 30–31 *see also* licence
long lease 22, 50–51

management:
  blocks of flats 67–8
  by local council 79
  tenants' association 67
mortgages:
  mortgagee's power of sale 88
  obtaining consent 69
  setting rent 72
multiple lets:
  fire prevention 58–9
  joint and several liability 48
  lease or licence? 49–50
  management 67–8
  overcrowding 47
  rent 47
  suitability of property 46

nuisance 57, 91, 109

oral contract 25, 76
overcrowding 47

periodic lease 20
periodic licence 31
Protection from Eviction Act (1977) 109–12

Ready reckoner 13–16
references of tenant/licensee 76

127

renewal of licence 32, 34
renewal of tenancy:
  change in circumstances 32, 34
  express periodic 97
  fixed term 96
  statutory periodic tenancy 98
rent:
  accepting rent after end of term 99
  arrears as ground for possession 90, 91
  assured tenancies and assured shortholds compared 40
  collection 70
  by agent 72
  default 101
  Department of Social Security paying rent 78
  ground rent 51
  increasing rent 79–83
  interest 102
  joint and several tenants 47
  'mesne profits' 100
  method of payment 73
  rent review clause 80
  security of tenure, effect on rent 40
  statutory periodic tenancies 40
  termination of tenancy and liability for rent 85, 95; *see also* Rent Assessment Committee
Rent Assessment Committee 23
  alteration of terms of agreement 98
  asessment of increase in rent 80–83
  assessment of rent 40, 41, 44, 73, 80, 82
repair and maintenance:
  'Acts of God' 54
  agent making repairs 72
  breach of covenant to repair 107–8
  delay in making repairs 54, 79, 110
  emergency repairs 77–8
  entering property to inspect condition 54, 79
  exterior repairs 53
  interior repairs 53
  Landlord and Tenant Act (1985) 53
  landlord's obligations 53
  licensoris and licensee's obligations 31, 37
  notice of repair 54, 79
  payment by tenant 53
  rent 53
  short leases 50
  standard 54–5
  tenant's fault 53, 108

tenant's obligations 52–3
vacation of property 95
waste or neglect 35
wear and tear 35

security and safety 28, 29, 33, 69, 58, 59, 63
security of tenure:
  agreement to surrender 85
  Landlord and Tenant Act (1954) 51
  licences 30, 73
  rent 40
seizing goods 105
service charge 63
  accounts 66
  alternatives 67
  default 103
  disputes 66–7
  level of charge 64
  rights of tenants 66
  standard of services 64
  what to charge for 64
  when to charge 65
  who to charge 64–5
short lease 22, 50
showing property 29, 69, 75–6, 94
'Small Claims Court' 103–4
solicitors:
  consulting 11–12, 71–2
  contribution to fees by tenant 71
specific performance 108
stamp duty 16
statutory periodic tenancy 39
  altering terms 98
  increasing rent 80, 82
  renewal 96, 98
  termination 39, 86, 93
sub-letting 34, 55–6, 87, 91
sureties 74

tenancy at sufferance 21
tenancy at will 21
tenant-like manner 52, 60
tenants:
  attracting the right tenant for the property 41, 46
  choosing tenants 29, 47, 75–7
  'DSS' tenants 78–9
  enforcing obligations 56
  friends of tenant 56
  moving in 77–8
  moving out 95–6
  references 76
termination:
  agreement to surrender 85

INDEX

break clause 42, 85
common law notice periods 84
default in rent 102
   Housing Act tenancy 106
   licences 22–23, 31, 108
   non-Housing Act tenancy 108
licences 99–100
multiple lets 48–9
nuisance 57
possession order 87
practical matters 94–6
termination by landlord:
   assured shorthold tenancies:
      fixed term 92
      notice 92–3
      periodic 93
      statutory periodic 93
   assured tenancies:
      fixed 86
      periodic 86
      statutory periodic 86
termination by tenant:
   effect 85
   fixed term 85
   notice 84
   periodic 85
   statutory periodic tenancy 85

use of property 57

warrant of execution 105
waste or neglect 35
wear and tear 55
writ of fieri facias *see* seizing goods